To

_____

From

_____

Date

_____

THE HEALING POWER OF

FORGIVENESS

EXPERIENCE PEACE *and*
RESTORED RELATIONSHIPS

GEORGE FOSTER

...inspired by life

© 2011 Ellie Claire™ Gift & Paper Corp.
a division of Worthy Media, Inc.
Brentwood, TN 37207
www.ellieclaire.com

THE HEALING POWER OF FORGIVENESS

Experience Peace and Restored Relationships
Copyright © 2011 by George Foster

ISBN 978-1-60936-125-9

Abridged from the American edition published in 2008 by Summerside Press,
Minneapolis, MN 55337, USA.

First published in 1993 in Portuguese as
Perdão Já! by Editora Betânia S/C
Caixa Postal 5010–31611-970 Venda Nova, MG, Brazil.

Subsequent editions in Portuguese titled
O Poder Restaurador do Perdão.
Translated by Myrian Tlitha Lins.

Stock or custom editions of Ellie Claire titles may be purchased in bulk
for educational, business, ministry, fundraising, or sales promotional
use. For information, please e-mail info@ellieclaire.com.

Design by Lookout Design

Printed in the USA.

TABLE OF CONTENTS

*"You will know the truth,
and truth will set you free."*

JOHN 8:32

Introduction

What I am seeking to offer you in this book is freedom from bitterness, resentment, and recurring feelings of worthlessness that come as an aftermath of the disappointment and pain you have suffered.

Forgiveness is not just a once-and-for-all emotion. It is a choice taken with God's help and a process of healing that enables you to be free— not from the memory but from the pain of your suffering.

After having made the decision to forgive, you should not have to experience ongoing guilt, self-accusation, and resentment.

*If you do not forgive men their sins,
your Father will not forgive your sins.*

MATTHEW 6:15

1

Forgive Or...

A seventeen-year-old girl once appeared on the Oprah Winfrey Show, facing the violent man who, four years earlier, had beaten her beyond recognition and left her to die. After seventeen operations for facial reconstruction, her words to the vicious attacker were, "I don't hate you. I hate what you did to me, and I have had to forgive you so I could go on with my life."

Before she ever got to the television studio, she had made the right decision—the intelligent, redemptive decision—that would enable her to not only face her attacker, but also to face life with peace of heart and emotional freedom from the suffering she had known.

Her decision wasn't an easy one; it was a difficult choice and would be a difficult one to maintain. It would require an ongoing healing process and a commitment to reaffirm her decision every time her suffering came to mind. Still, her future was opened in a way she would have never known had she not decided to forgive.

We all get hurt

Few of us will ever face what this young woman has, but we have our own issues! We have our hurts. We have our complaints. In a world filled with conflict and pain, it is almost certain that you and I have been—or will be—deceived, injured, cheated, betrayed, slighted, rejected, or in some other way hurt. Then what?

Unless we forgive the ones who hurt us, we could find ourselves emotionally and spiritually crippled for the rest of our lives. An act of forgiveness can be the decisive step in solving both emotional and physical problems.

Forgiveness is the effective solution for relationship issues both in our personal lives and in society. The ability to forgive, keep on forgiving, *and know we have forgiven* is a constant challenge. More than that, it is an attainable source of strength and peace!

Forgiveness may be the most difficult gift we can offer to anyone, and, ironically, it must be offered to those who least deserve it—aggressors, offenders, and injurers, whether intentional or not. And here's the twist: We do it for our own good!

My interest in the subject of forgiveness is both personal and pastoral—personal because I, too, have been betrayed, and pastoral because I have been called upon to help people with their issues of bitterness and pain. The willingness to forgive brings God's help into situations that seem overwhelming and hopeless.

An overnight ride with a betrayer

One cold night I rode an overnight sleeper bus from São Paulo, Brazil, where I had been on business, to that nation's third largest city, Belo Horizonte, where I lived. It was my second straight night on the bus, and though I should have been able to sleep, I could not.

Instead, I agonized over a betrayal I had suffered by a person whom I called a friend. I struggled with angry, bitter thoughts toward him. I had already decided to forgive him, but my decision was made too hastily without much thought for what he had done and without reflection on how deeply I felt the pain. I had tried to forgive out of a sense of Christian duty based on the following logic: He betrayed me. I am a Christian. Christians forgive; therefore I forgive him.

Now it came back to haunt me. That night as I lay in the reclining seat—unable to sleep, to get up, to think of anything but the disloyalty I had suffered—I realized that the man who had hurt me was traveling with me. In fact, for several weeks he rarely left my thoughts or emotions. I often felt angry and resentful. If he had suddenly appeared on the bus in person, something might have happened that a missionary pastor should not be a part of!

Then I heard the silent-but-persistent voice of Satan, "the accuser," saying, "If you had truly forgiven him, you wouldn't feel the way you do now!"

So not only did I feel hurt and angry, I felt sinful and condemned for not forgiving. (Have you been there before?) Seeking to be rational, I said to myself, "Well, if I haven't forgiven him before, I forgive him now!"

That was helpful for a time, but it didn't answer my confusion regarding *decisions* to forgive and concurrent *feelings* of unforgiveness. I thought that the decision to forgive would somehow work in me the miracle of instant and permanent freedom from the pain I felt. Believe me, it didn't. Every time I allowed myself to think about what this person had done, I relived the emotions and anger returned to my heart. So I had to be careful what I thought, what I said, and what I did.

The truth we need

Many Bible texts teach us to control our thoughts, words, and actions. Ephesians 4:29–32 says,

....

Do not let any unwholesome talk come out of your mouths,
but only what is helpful for building others up according to
their needs, that it may benefit those who listen. And do not
grieve the Holy Spirit of God, with whom you were sealed
for the day of redemption. Get rid of all bitterness, rage
and anger, brawling and slander, along with every form of
malice. Be kind and compassionate to one another, forgiving
each other, just as in Christ God forgave you.

....

God's Word tells us what to do, what to say, and
even what to think about, but it does not tell us what
we should feel. It was liberating for me to understand
that feelings are essentially *involuntary reactions or responses*
to actions, words, thoughts, and happenings. We should
never accept condemnation based purely upon our
feelings. We can only control our feelings by doing,
saying, and thinking what is right.

Why forgiveness?

Unless we forgive, we experience ongoing anger,
bitterness, conflict, dysfunction, and hostility, along
with mental and emotional instability and possible
physical illness. Ironically, we may experience more
pain from our ongoing attitudes than we did from the
offense that originated the pain. We may experience

much more pain than the person we are trying to punish by refusing to forgive them.

As I consider the need for forgiveness, I like to follow this sequence of realities:

1. We live in a world that brings us trouble and conflict. "In this world you will have trouble. But take heart! I have overcome the world" (John 16:33). The kingdom of darkness conflicts with God's kingdom of light. Depending upon the stage of our journey from darkness to light, we may experience confusion.

2. We may be betrayed or attacked or offended or wronged or wounded. Brother will betray brother, a father his children, and children their parents (see Matthew 10:21). Mistakes, accidents, and tragedies happen, sometimes with nothing or no one to blame. Sometimes we suffer while doing right and others prosper while doing wrong.

3. To recover, we must fully forgive those who wound us. "If you forgive men...your heavenly Father will also forgive you" (Matthew 6:14). Forgiveness is the tool for repairing our battered emotions. We may wish to be free from individuals who hurt us, but they only leave our troubled spirits in peace once we forgive them.

4. Severe pain is hard to forgive. "How many times must I forgive?" (Matthew 18:21 NCV). We may experience more pain from ongoing, unforgiving attitudes than we did from the offense that first originated the pain.

5. Forgiveness must reach each injured person. "Be kind and compassionate to one another, forgiving each other" (Ephesians 4:32). We must forgive those who hurt us, ask forgiveness of those we hurt, and forgive ourselves.

6. Not just a feeling, forgiveness is a decision, a commitment, and a process. How many times do we forgive? "Seventy times seven!" (i.e., countless times). (See Matthew 18:22.) We must free offenders of emotional debts and work on our inner reactions until we, too, are free.

7. Jesus set the example and the standard by forgiving those who crucified Him. "Father, forgive them, for they do not know what they are doing" (Luke 23:34). As we receive forgiveness in Christ, we must offer forgiveness to others as He did to us.

8. Most importantly, Jesus can empower us to forgive as He did. "I can do all things through Christ who strengthens me" (Philippians 4:13 NKJV). God's Spirit pours His love into our hearts and enables us to love and forgive. We must ask and believe.

9. We recover peace, joy, and stability as we obtain and maintain a forgiving spirit. "Forgiving each other, just as in Christ God forgave you" (Ephesians 4:32). We set aside our grievances and leave them there.

10. **We are called to be God's instruments of forgiveness, peace, and reconciliation.** "He has committed to us the message of reconciliation" (2 Corinthians 5:19). Our experiences of peace and freedom affect those around us.

Relationships: rich or risky?

When I was in college, visiting missionaries spoke about problems we might face in cross-cultural mission settings. They were especially interested in warning us about issues that could cause missionaries to give up and leave the field—a major concern to every missionary organization. Typically the speakers would say: "Your biggest problem will not be the culture, language, food, customs, or climate.. Your major difficulty will be getting along with your missionary colleagues."

Quite frankly, I didn't believe them. Let me make it clear: *I do believe them now!* I have believed them for forty years—ever since I went to the mission field and, three weeks after my arrival, found myself in a disagreement with one of my colleagues.

We like to talk about lofty spiritual subjects such as

— loving God and loving our neighbors as ourselves, as directed in Luke 10:27;
— achieving unity in the body of Christ to increase the effectiveness of our work and to set an

example to a world that needs to believe;
— having peaceful relationships with family and friends.

Let's face it: None of this is possible unless we learn to offer and receive forgiveness. Even though the need for forgiveness is easily understood and the principles are well known, the practical applications are subjective and filled with emotional distress.

I am not a trained psychologist. I have spent my adult life as a pastor and am now a pastor to pastors and missionaries. But, I have learned that everyone needs to be forgiven and needs to forgive. Everyone needs to learn more about forgiveness and make it a permanent, restorative part of their daily lives.

God wants you to be a forgiven and forgiving person. He calls you to it, holds you to it, and will empower you to do it.

forgive us our debts,
as we also have forgiven our debtors.

MATTHEW 6:12

Be Forgiven
and Be Forgiving

When *The Passion of Christ* hit the theaters, everyone talked about the violence. My wife, Dolly, and I wanted to see the film, but we weren't looking forward to all the bloodshed. We decided to wait awhile before making up our minds.

Then one night our son called from São Paulo, Brazil, where he lives with his wife. "Dad, you have to see this film!" he said.

Curious about his enthusiasm, I asked, "Why is that?"

His answer was surprising and convincing: "It made me feel that I never want to do anything wrong again." We made immediate plans to attend.

After the showing, Dolly and I left the theater in silence, both impacted by the vivid scenes. Later Dolly said, "What got to me was when Jesus was undergoing such suffering and He said, 'Father, forgive them; for they know not what they do'" (Luke 23:34 KJV).

Forgiveness is the issue

Why all that suffering? The Lord Jesus Christ, God's Son, came into this world to take upon Himself the sin and suffering of all humanity and make atonement for us on the cross—so that we could be forgiven, healed, and restored to a relationship with God. That's the gospel truth! Jesus does not ask us to atone for our sins or for the sins of others, but He does ask us to offer forgiveness to those who sin against us just as He offers forgiveness to us. From His point of view, the forgiveness we receive and the forgiveness we offer are linked. It's as if He keeps repeating, "We are forgiven, so we forgive" and "We forgive, so we are forgiven."

Jesus spoke in surprising ways about forgiveness. His teaching is extremely vivid and demanding. Consider the force of the following verses:

....

And when you stand praying, if you hold anything against anyone, forgive him, so that your Father in heaven may forgive you your sins (Mark 11:25).

If your brother sins, rebuke him, and if he repents, forgive him. If he sins against you seven times in a day, and seven times comes back to you and says, "I repent," forgive him (Luke 17:3–4).

....

Receiving forgiveness

In Luke 5:17–26, Jesus was teaching in His hometown of Nazareth and, as He taught, people in the crowd were being healed of their sicknesses and diseases. Seeing this, four village men thought of their paralytic friend and carried him to the meeting, hoping he might be healed.

Arriving at the house where Jesus was teaching, they encountered a crowd so tightly packed that they were not able to get in. Desperately they climbed to the rooftop, calculated where Jesus was standing below, pulled off the roof tiles, and lowered their friend on a mat into the presence of the Lord.

It's possible that everyone present knew about his paralysis. Only Jesus seemed to perceive and care about a deeper need. The crowd was shocked when Jesus, instead of pronouncing words of healing, said, "Friend, your sins are forgiven" (verse 20 NCV).

Religious leaders objected and commented among themselves that Jesus was being blasphemous. No one could forgive sins except God. Then Jesus said to the paralyzed man, "Stand up, take your mat, and go home" (verse 4 NCV). To everyone's amazement, the man stood to his feet and walked out—healed and forgiven!

What wonderful insights we find in this story. It tells us that...

1. More than physical healing, our greatest need is forgiveness. That man may have been reconciled to lying on that mat for the rest of his life but could not bear living another minute without being reconciled to God. We all have sinned. We all need forgiveness.

2. Jesus Christ has the authority to forgive our sins. You and I can forgive people for what they do to us, but only Jesus can offer the pardon to establish or restore our right-standing before God.

3. When Jesus forgives us, He loves to assure us that we are forgiven. He often chose clear words to let people know they were forgiven:

....

Friend, your sins are forgiven (Luke 5:20).
Neither do I condemn you; go and sin no more
(John 8:11 NKJV).
Today you will be with me in paradise (Luke 23:43).
Your faith has saved you; go in peace (Luke 7:50).

....

Jesus still loves to unequivocally assure us that our sins are forgiven.

4. With forgiveness, we may also experience physical and emotional healing. Many illnesses of the body and mind are directly related to problems of the spirit and soul. Dealing with the spiritual issues often brings breakthroughs in the physical realm.

5. No problem is too hard for Jesus. Jesus made it clear that He had the authority and power to declare, "You are forgiven" and "Get up and walk." Nothing is too hard for Him.

6. The best thing we can do is to get into the presence of Jesus. Wonderful things can happen in Christ's presence when we look to Him and have faith.

Nothing is more important than to tend to than the salvation of our eternal souls. Maybe we assume that we are forgiven because we're nice people. Or perhaps we just hope we are forgiven. Jesus wants to give us the strong biblical assurance that we are forgiven. All of us would love to hear the words "Friend, your sins are forgiven" directly from the lips of Jesus. It's an assurance we can have.

Offering forgiveness to others

Jesus taught His disciples that it is not enough to be forgiven; they must also forgive: "If you forgive men when they sin against you, your heavenly Father will also forgive you. But if you do not forgive men their sins, your Father will not forgive your sins" (Matthew 6:14).

An unforgiving heart can't truly receive forgiveness. Jesus spelled out the connection between forgiveness received and forgiveness offered in a dialogue with Peter in Matthew 18:21–22. This impulsive disciple may have been tired of the offenses a colleague committed and asked, "Lord, how many times shall I forgive my brother when he sins against me? Up to seven times?"

Jesus answered, "I tell you, not seven times, but seventy-seven times." This number simply means as many times as is necessary.

Then Jesus went on to illustrate his point with a story.

....

The kingdom of heaven is like a king who wanted to settle accounts with his servants. As he began the settlement, a man who owed him ten thousand talents was brought to him. Since he was not able to pay, the master ordered that he and his wife and his children and all that he had be sold to repay the debt.

The servant fell on his knees before him. "Be patient with me," he begged, "and I will pay back everything." The servant's master took pity on him, canceled the debt and let him go.

But when that servant went out, he found one of his fellow servants who owed him a hundred denarii. He grabbed him and began to choke him. "Pay back what you owe me!" he demanded.

His fellow servant fell to his knees and begged him, "Be patient with me, and I will pay you back."

But he refused. Instead, he went off and had the man thrown into prison until he could pay the debt. When the other servants saw what had happened, they were greatly distressed and went and told their master everything that had happened.

Then the master called the servant in. "You wicked servant," he said, "I canceled all that debt of yours because you begged me to. Shouldn't you have had mercy on your fellow servant just as I had on you?" In anger his master turned him over to the jailers to be tortured, until he should pay back all he owed.

This is how my heavenly Father will treat each of you unless you forgive your brother from your heart (Matthew 18:23–35).

....

Isn't it incredible that a man could be forgiven such a large debt and then refuse to forgive such a small one!

Do you suppose that he

— didn't understand that he was fully and forever forgiven,

— thought he would have to pay at a later date? (He offered),

— thought he could pay by his own schemes,

- thought he should make a token effort to pay,
- was too proud to admit how poor and helpless he was,
- had other debts he had never revealed,
- distrusted the character of the king?

Debt-free living

This man had a fresh start, but he wasn't prepared for it. The same greed that had put him into debt now motivated him to demand an insignificant amount from a colleague. Not only did his attitude injure his colleague, it brought about his own imprisonment and torture.

What kind of torture do we experience when we don't forgive? Author and pastor David Seamands explains that when we fail to forgive, we often suffer from hidden tormentors like sickness, guilt, mental distress, insomnia, eating disorders, chemical dependence, self-hatred, self-destructive behavior, and personal conflicts.[1]

Let's talk about debt

In the Lord's Prayer we are taught to pray, "Forgive us our sins [debts], for we also forgive everyone who sins against us [debtors]" (Luke 11:4). Paul instructs us, "Give everyone what you owe him: If you owe taxes, pay taxes; if revenue, then revenue; if respect, then respect; if honor, then honor. Let no debt remain outstanding, except the continuing debt to love one another" (Romans 13:7–8).

To the degree we become aware of and appreciate the forgiveness we receive, we increase in our own ability to forgive. Mercy begets mercy. Those who have experienced the mercy and forgiveness of God are qualified and become responsible to offer that mercy to others. If this story tells us anything, it is that for our own good and for our personal freedom, we must forgive those who have debts they owe us. I don't think that means we should cancel all business debts that people owe (although that may sometimes be appropriate) but we should cancel all records and resentment of offenses.

Yes, the person may have a debt to pay, but we have a debt as well. As the apostle so clearly states, if we have experienced the love of God, we have a debt of love to pay to everyone: "Since God so loved us, we also ought to love one another" (1 John 4:11).

It's not a trade-off. We don't love to pay for love. We don't forgive to pay for forgiveness. We love and forgive in response to the love and forgiveness we have received. The forgiveness we offer is an indicator that we truly have been healthily forgiven. If we find ourselves unwilling to forgive, perhaps we need to make sure that we have fully accepted the forgiveness that Christ offers to us. This is not something we can earn or deserve; it is something that we must humbly and gratefully receive.

However we look at it, the challenge to forgive people who hurt us is one that—with God's help—we can rise to and achieve. The more we experience the love and forgiveness of God, the better equipped we will be to love and forgive others.

If we confess our sins, he...will forgive.

1 John 1:9

Forgiveness for the Forgiven

When I lived in Brazil and wrote magazine articles in Portuguese, a troubled young man wrote to me. Here's the translation of his letter:

I have a problem. Four months ago my girlfriend and I were converted to Christ. Before our conversion, we had sex together regularly. Since then we have tried to stop, but several times we have fallen. Each time I feel guilty and angry at myself, but it happens again and again.

I sought counsel with our pastor, and he told me to confess my sin before the whole church. It was very hard, but I did what he said and my happiness returned. Sadly, though, within a week, we sinned again. At that point I thought there was no hope for me and that I might as well go back to the life I had lived before. But I know that is exactly what Satan wants. One night I told my girlfriend how I felt—that if the Lord should come for me, I wouldn't be ready.

What I want you to answer is this: Has God forgiven us? Sometimes I think God doesn't love us. I'm afraid He will punish me, I often feel like a worthless animal.

Please be frank with me. After confessing Christ and falling into sin again, is there forgiveness for us? Is our name written in the Book of Life? I beg an answer of you.

....

I remember thinking, *There is something about the honesty of this young man that I like!* No excuses. No blaming the other person—or anyone else! I took time to write him the answer I thought he deserved and certainly needed.

First, though, I addressed the issue confessing their sin before the whole church. Scripture does say: "Confess your sins to each other and pray for each other so that you may be healed" (James 5:16). Public confession may be necessary when the offender is a church leader and public knowledge of the offense compromises the testimony of the church. But since this young couple's sins were private, confessing before the entire church certainly didn't do any lasting good. I wish the pastor had been guided by the rule of thumb I like to follow: Make the confession as public as the sin was.

Behind the questions

These questions may have been behind the ones the young man asked and that many Christians also ask.

1. Am I forgiven if can't stop sinning?
2. Am I forgiven if don't feel forgiven?
3. Is God angry with me?
4. Does He still love and accept me?
5. Have I committed the unpardonable sin?

In the head or heart

The short answers are these:

1. Who says you can't stop sinning? God can provide the grace to help you change.
2. Being forgiven doesn't depend on feeling forgiven.
3. No, I believe that God feels compassion and extends mercy to you.
4. God's mercy exists to bring you to repentance and victory.
5. You haven't committed "the unpardonable sin"!

My letter of response included all of these statements. I have observed, however, that many Christians theoretically accept answers like these but can't believe and apply them. Doubt and shame plague countless believers—even though they have prayed for forgiveness once, twice, a thousand times. They *hope* they are forgiven. They *say* they are forgiven. But in their hearts they are not sure.

A few years ago, I was part of a group of people who counseled a young woman who had served as a missionary in India. She left India because she thought she had committed the "unpardonable sin"—though she would never tell us what it was. A dedicated group of Christians prayed for her and supported her. She seemed to cling to our prayers but couldn't embrace our counsel in her heart. Tragically, she lost hope and, to our horror, took her own life.

Once I was in Europe, speaking to a group of young missionaries. An attractive young woman in the group had taken a vacation, met a former boyfriend, and plunged into two weeks of sexual encounters. When her vacation was over, she returned to her mission work. She was willing to do her "Christian duty" but feared that she would never again have true fellowship with God. When God's Word convinced her that there is forgiveness and restoration for those who practice even shameful behavior, she repented and believed that her fellowship with God was restored.

Why did she feel her sin so deeply? Let me say what many people don't want to hear: She felt guilt and shame because she *needed* to feel guilty, and she *needed* to be ashamed of what she had done. She was created to feel that way after committing the sins she did. It was this conviction that made it possible for her to feel the same depth of repentance, forgiveness, and cleansing once she responded to God's grace! I'm convinced that she had a life-changing experience of forgiveness and cleansing that brought her the strength to overcome new temptations. She was like the woman to whom Jesus said, "Go and sin no more" (John 8:11 NKJV).

Really converted to Christ?

Some Christians can't believe that people who commit these kinds of sin have truly been converted to Christ. Others think that if they ever were converted, they have abandoned or lost their faith—especially the girl who ended her own life. Only God truly knows.

Each of them had moral breakdowns and deep psychological and spiritual needs, but they were seeking help to put their lives back in order. They were not casual or flippant about their sins or their confessions. They wanted to follow Christ. They hated what they had done. They struggled against their temptations, sought to find a way back, and desperately and humbly asked for help. Tragically, one of them gave up the fight.

God's view of sin in a believer's life

God has provided abundant life through faith in Jesus

Christ—and that abundant life includes ample victory over sin.

The Good News is better than most people believe. We can be freed from both the *penalty* and the *power* of sin. Scripture promises, "Sin will not be your master, because you are not under law but under God's grace" (Romans 6:14 NCV). God's grace has the power to keep us from sinning. God provides a way of escape from temptation so that we do not have to fall (1 Corinthians 10:13).

Transaction or transformation?

I hear people speak of salvation as though it were a business deal—a transaction rather than a transformation. In exchange for a moment of decision and a simple prayer, you are entitled to eternal life. Just say the magic words *I accept you, Jesus, as my Savior*—and the deal is cut. Your sins are forgiven—past, present, and future—and you are now a child of God.

Once you've prayed that prayer and made that deal, you can pretty much do as you please. Don't let your religion interfere with your fun. If you sin, don't sweat it; you can always confess If you fall, you claim 1 John 1:9: "If we confess our sins, he will…forgive us our sins."

This wonderful promise is both used and abused. It brings us reassurance when we are deeply convicted of sin and truly repent of the wrong we have done. There are times, though, when confession is made superficially, maybe even flippantly—*Oops, God, sorry 'bout that.* The trouble with that casual approach is that neither God nor the offender is fooled. We can only know and feel we are forgiven when our repentance is real.

Hanging over hell

At the other extreme is a much tougher approach: To make sure you acquire the proper fear of God, some leaders hold you over the brink of hell until you nearly despair. They show you your sins in detail along with your deserved destination. You are told that you are a helpless sinner of no value. If, however, you humbly identify yourself as scum, you are shown the way of escape through rigorous repentance. Then you are kept in the fold by reminders of how unworthy you are, how demanding God is, and what grave danger you face if you sin again.

Biblical balance

The examples above are extreme but not uncommon. The book of 1 John gives a more balanced view.

1. No one is exempt from the possibility of sinning (1:8).
2. It is never God's will for us to sin (2:1).

3. Sin is an intruder—not an invited resident in the Christian's life (3:6).
4. If we claim to not sin but do not obey truth, we fool ourselves (1:8).
5. If we go on willfully practicing sin, we are not saved (3:6).
6. We may stumble or struggle with compulsive behavior but not deliberately live a sinful life (3:9).
7. If we sin, Jesus represents us to the Father, so that—through repentance and faith—we may continue to receive his grace and walk in his fellowship (2:1–2).
8. If we repent and confess our sins, God forgives and cleanses us (1:9).

Paul brings up an issue in his letter to the Romans: "So do you think we should continue sinning so that God will give us even more grace? No! We died to our old sinful lives, so how can we continue living with sin?" (Romans 6:1–2 NCV).

Not only does God's grace (unmerited favor and empowerment) provide forgiveness for our weaknesses, there is mercy for compulsive wrong behavior. Even deliberate sinful choices can be fully forgiven. The method: "If we confess our sins, he will forgive our sins, because we can trust God to do what is right.

He will cleanse us from all the wrongs we have done"
(I John 1:9 NCV).

Be specific!

Pastor T. A. Hegre was my teacher and pastor for many years. An observant traveler, he told simple stories to illustrate truth. One story reminded us that the confession of sin must always be specific, never generalized.

In India he saw women washing their clothes by soaking them in the river and beating them on rocks. As he watched, a friend told him about a woman who once let her clothes remain soiled for so long that she was embarrassed to open her bundle. To avoid exposure, she immersed the whole bundle in the water and then beat it on the rocks. Her clothes shook around a bit but did not get clean.

Pastor Hegre pointed out that sins are committed one by one and should be confessed one by one. When we sincerely confess and forsake our sins, God cleanses us.

To confess is to agree with God about the rightness or wrongness of what we have thought or said or done or failed to do. When we know we are wrong, we must admit our guilt. Remember these words of Scripture: "If you hide your sins, you will not succeed. If you confess and reject them [or forsake them], you will receive mercy" (Proverbs 28:13 NCV).

Victory, yes!
Sinless perfection, no!

Christ's blood cleanses us from all sin (1 John 1.7). His Word says, "sin will not be your master, because you are not under law, but under grace" (Romans 6:14). We can know that no sin, is too dirty or too deeply rooted for God to cleanse and remove. The issue is not whether we will ever stumble into another sin, but will we daily yield our lives to Christ and allow Him to make us the Christians that God wants us to be? Will we be clean, victorious, fruitful, and Spirit-filled?

"Who told you that you were naked?"

4

Do You Really Think It's Concealed?

When our daughter Marci was three years old, she would lie in bed for her daily nap and sing Sunday school songs before dropping off to sleep.

One afternoon, however, Marci didn't sing. For Dolly, Marci's silence seemed louder than her songs. After awhile Dolly checked to see what was happening. To her surprise, she saw Bible pages pasted on every wall.

Why this sudden interest in displaying God's Word? Marci had used her coloring crayons to draw pictures on the wall. Then she realized that Mommy wasn't going to like this, so she tore out several pages of her brother's Bible and carefully pasted them over the colorful drawings. She hoped she would be safe—after all, her deeds were covered with the Word of God! When Dolly entered the room, Marci discovered an important Bible principle: "He who conceals his sins does not prosper, but whoever confesses and renounces them finds mercy" (Proverbs 28:13).

We have told this story more times than Marci would like to hear and have laughed at the foolishness of her childish attempts to hide her transgression. She did apologize, and she did find mercy.

Adult cover-ups

How foolish children can be in their attempts to hide their wrongdoing! But their foolishness does not compare with the excuses that are made, the blaming that is done, and the cover-ups attempted by adults.

These attempts go back to Eden where Adam and Eve disobeyed God's command in Genesis 3. They could eat of all the fruit in the garden, except the forbidden fruit. You know the story. They looked, they desired, they ate, and suddenly they were ashamed. For the first time they put clothes on their bodies and hid from their Creator.

The shame and blame game

We have all rationalized, excused, disguised, and called our errors by another name, or we have blamed other people. We think that the worst thing that could possibly happen is to be exposed for who we are and what we have done.

When politicians are caught in transgressions, they may admit making "bad choices" but hasten to assure us that their choices don't really reflect who they are. Jesus, of course, would disagree. "What comes out of a man is what makes him 'unclean.' For from within, out of men's hearts, come evil thoughts, sexual immorality, theft, murder, adultery, greed, malice, deceit, lewdness, envy, slander, arrogance and folly." (Mark 7:20–22). "No good tree bears bad fruit, nor does a bad tree bear good fruit" (Luke 6:43).

Adam and Eve didn't need to learn the cover-up technique. It came naturally to them. It comes naturally to us. We want people to think well of us. We want to think well of ourselves. We protect our reputation from the inner voice of conscience and especially from the searching of the Holy Spirit.

2 Samuel 11 recounts the stupidity and cruelty practiced by David, normally the wise and trustworthy king described as a man after God's own heart (Acts 13:22).

One spring season, rather than going to battle, David stayed home and sent his armed forces out with Commander Joab. One sleepless night, David walked the terrace roof of the palace.

To his surprise, David saw a beautiful woman

bathing, probably on one of the other rooftops. Instead of going inside, he continued watching.

When David asked about the gorgeous woman, a servant said her name was Bathsheba. The servant then gently reminded David that she was married to Uriah, a faithful soldier away at war.

Fascination turned to desire, desire to lust, lust to a bad decision. David sent messengers to get her.

When Bathsheba returned home, David thought he had gotten by with something.

But he heard from her again. Bathsheba was pregnant. Then David set to scheming again. "Send me Uriah the Hittite" (verse 6).

Everything will look normal, David thought. *I'll ask for a report on the war and then send Uriah home to sleep with his wife. Everyone will think the child is his.*

But David was not counting on Uriah's extreme loyalty. Uriah didn't think it was fair to enjoy a night with his wife when all his colleagues slept in tents on battle alert. He slept outdoors that night.

David tried again the next evening. He invited Uriah for drinks and sent him home again. Again Uriah refused, so David sent him back to the war with instructions written to Joab: "Put Uriah in the front line where the fighting is fiercest" (verse 15).

This time the plan worked. Uriah was killed in battle, and David took Bathsheba as his wife. "But the thing David had done displeased the LORD" (verse 27).

The blessing of getting caught

Sure, David kept his sin from the public for a while, but he could not hide from the voice of his conscience or from the voice of God. His sin caught up with him when the prophet Nathan came and told him what is now a well-known story.

....

There were two men in a city. One was rich, but the other was poor. The rich man had many sheep and cattle. But the poor man had nothing except one little female lamb he had bought. The poor man fed the lamb, and it grew up with5 him and his children. It shared his food and drank from his cup and slept in his arms. The lamb was like a daughter to him. Then a traveler stopped to visit the rich man. The rich man wanted to feed the traveler, but he didn't want to take one of his own sheep or cattle. Instead, he took the lamb from the poor man and cooked it for his visitor (2 Samuel 12:1–4 NCV).

....

David was furious with the man and demanded he pay for the lamb four times over.

How righteous David sounds. He sympathizes with the poor shepherd and condemns the offender—until the faithful prophet points his finger at David and says in verse 7, "You are the man!" Until that moment, David felt that to be discovered was the worst thing that could happen to him. He later rejoiced in the clean break he was able to make once he was caught.

....

Blessed is he whose transgressions are forgiven, whose sins are covered.... I acknowledged my sin to you and did not cover up my iniquity. I said, "I will confess my transgressions to the Lord"—and you forgave the guilt of my sin (Psalm 32:1, 5).

....

David suffered for his sin in many ways, including through the death of the child, but—once he came clean—the gnawing voice of his troubled conscience was silenced. His time of dryness was over, and his strength was renewed. Later, instead of hiding his faults, David would pray in Psalm 139:23-24, "Search me, O God, and know my heart; test me and know my anxious thoughts. See if there is any offensive way in me, and lead me in the way everlasting."

God's perspective on conscience

What is conscience? It's the sense of what is right or wrong in one's behavior or motives—an inner arbitrator that approves or disapproves of thoughts, deeds, and attitudes. In the Judeo-Christian tradition, it's the inner sense of whether one is pleasing God and living up to His standards. Although the word rarely appears in the Old Testament, it is sprinkled liberally throughout the New Testament.

When Paul appeared before the Roman governor Felix he said, "I strive always to keep my conscience clear before God and man" (Acts 24:16).

Paul did not necessarily equate the voice of the conscience to the voice of the Holy Spirit. He once admitted, "My conscience is clear, but that does not make me innocent. It is the Lord who judges me" (1 Corinthians 4:4).

John described the conflict that can exist between the voice of conscience and the voice of God.

....

This then is...how we set our hearts at rest in his presence whenever our hearts condemn us. For God is greater than our hearts, and he knows everything.... If our hearts do not condemn us, we have confidence before God (1 John 3:19–22).

....

Paul warned believers not to hurt those who are too sensitive: "When you sin against your brothers in this way and wound their weak conscience, you sin against Christ" (1 Corinthians 8:12).

The conscience, Paul inferred, is not the final answer, because we don't all think alike: "Why should my freedom be judged by another's conscience?" (1 Corinthians 10:29).

Still, it is important to take good care of the conscience. It is formed by the moral and ethical training we receive, and it must be followed.

Paul wrote to his younger disciple Timothy: "The goal of this command is love, which comes from a pure heart and a good conscience and a sincere faith" (I Timothy 1:5).

He put this in stronger language and reemphasized it later in the same chapter.

I give you this instruction...so that...you may fight the good fight, holding on to faith and a good conscience. Some have rejected these and so have shipwrecked their faith (I Timothy 1:18–19).

An unforgettable lesson

In college, I learned that Christians need to get their consciences clean and keep them clean. During a prayer retreat, I heard college men apologize to one another for wrong attitudes and words. It emphasized to me that no one has peace of heart and mind unless he or she keeps clear accounts with God and other people.

As I grew in my Christian life, I made a list of several people whom I had offended or wronged in my teenage years. One by one I made things right with them. One offense, though, troubled me more than the others.

When my friend Lloyd heard I was studying for the ministry, he began to help me in any way he could. He sent books and a few modest cash gifts. Most importantly, whenever I came home on break from college, he loaned me his car.

Since I had owned a couple of cars by then, Lloyd assumed I had a valid driver's license. I didn't have one and I remained silent. Fortunately no problems occurred, even though I used his car several times.

Later, when I attempted to pray more effectively and become more intimate with God, I often thought about the way I had deceived Lloyd. I knew I should confess to him that I had used his car under false pretenses, but I rationalized that nothing had happened and that confessing would only destroy our friendship.

Finally it became so hard to pray that I negotiated with God. "I don't think I should tell him. But if You want me to, bring us together in a way that is so obviously not prearranged that I will know that is what You want (as if I didn't already know).

Soon after that prayer a famous evangelist came to town, and I decided to attend his meeting. I made my way toward the front of the auditorium looking for an empty seat, but none were available. Finally I walked along the front row until I saw one empty seat in the crowd—right beside Lloyd.

I felt a simultaneous rush of excitement and fear when Lloyd waved for me to sit with him. God had me where

He wanted me, and I knew that I couldn't hesitate. So I sat down and cleared my conscience and rediscovered an ease in prayer that I had not known for some time. I also acquired an enormous motivation to be honest in my dealings with people, a lesson that has served me well.

The way of the cross

There are simple sentences that we hate to say:

I was wrong. We don't mind saying, "I might not have been totally correct," or "Maybe that wasn't the best thing to do." But "I was wrong" is the confession we need to make.

I'm sorry. It's no good to recognize guilt if we don't express sorrow and repentance.

Please forgive me. This requires humility. We cannot assume a posture of superiority when we ask forgiveness.[1]

Why do we avoid these three sentences? Often it's because of three deceptive ideas:

1. The other person should make the first move.
2. If I repent and he doesn't, the situation won't change.
3. If humble myself, he will feel certain he is right.

If you are living with one or more of these ideas, may I remind you of three facts:

1. Jesus knew we were entirely to blame, but He made the first move toward us.
2. Jesus was baptized as though He were a common sinner.
3. Jesus humbled himself and was obedient unto death.

So I ask you, why shouldn't we go the way of the cross?

What to make right?

Some time ago I shortened and adapted the following list of questions from a Web site published by author and speaker Winkie Pratney. (You can read more about Winkie at winkiepratney.com.) This list is not meant to make you overly introspective but should instead help you to make your heart right with God.

Stealing—Have you taken money or property that was not yours?

Cheating—Have you gotten things from someone unfairly or dishonestly?

Lying—Have you practiced deception for selfish reasons?

Slander—Have you talked critically about people behind their backs?

Immorality—Have you failed to keep your body and mind pure?

Envy—Have you criticized others and exalted yourself?

Pride—Have you projected an untrue image of yourself?

Ingratitude—Have you taken the help of other people for granted?

Anger—Have you shown impatience with someone?

Cursing—Have you used vulgar language?

Habits—Are you a slave to food, drink, or stimulants?

Laziness—Have you shirked your share of responsibility?

Hindrance—Have you prevented others from doing God's work?

Hypocrisy—Has your falseness discouraged others from serving God?

Broken Vows—Have you made vows to God and not kept them? (If it was an unwise vow, ask for forgiveness and release.)

Walk in the light

Drop your self-deceit. Face your sin and turn from it with all your heart.

Once you have received forgiveness from the Lord, ask Him for the courage to confess to those you've wronged and the wisdom to know how to go about restoring your relationship. Confession is humbling yourself and admitting you're wrong. Restitution is preparing to pay back or restore wherever possible.

Your conscience must be clean before both God and man if you want to know peace and true freedom.

You do not have to confess every sin you have committed to everyone you know; but you should confess to individuals the specific sins you have committed against them. When you have cleared your conscience before God and man, you can trust God to fully restore your peace of heart and mind.

You intended to harm me,
but God intended it for good.

GENESIS 50:20

CHAPTER

5

They Plotted Evil!

The Bible records extraordinary and inspiring examples of forgiveness.

When Jesus said, "Father, forgive them, for they do not know what they are doing" in Luke 23:34, He set the standard and the example for all of us to follow.

Stephen, the first Christian martyr, took this example to heart when he faced religious leaders and accused them of betraying and murdering Jesus. They became furious and stoned him. With his final breath Stephen prayed, "Lord, do not hold this sin against them" (Acts 7:60).

Joseph is a third impressive biblical model. Let's look into his story starting in Genesis 37.

As a boy, Joseph was so much the favorite among

Jacob's sons that his ten elder brothers became extremely angry and jealous. He was bright, protected, and tattled to his father about the wrong things his brothers did.

They hated him for it.

Already a spoiled child, Joseph was given a special multicolored robe that set him apart from the others. What really got to his brothers was that Joseph was a dreamer. Every time Joseph talked about his dreams, he implied his elder brothers would be his servants.

When Joseph was about seventeen and his shepherd brothers were away tending the family flocks, Jacob sent him to see how they were doing. As he approached, the brothers decided to kill him. When a group of traveling Ishmaelite merchants appeared, Judah suggested they sell Joseph as a slave. The merchants, in turn, took Joseph to Egypt and sold him to Potiphar, the captain of the royal guard of Egypt.

Joseph humiliated

Once in Potiphar's house, Joseph proved to be an able administrator. He was such a loyal person of integrity that Potiphar entrusted to him the care of his entire household. Everybody admired him, including Potiphar's wife, who began to invite him to her bedroom for sex. After he refused several invitations, she grabbed him and desperately thrust herself upon him. He ran from her room, but unfortunately left his coat behind.

Angered by his refusal, Potiphar's wife accused him of trying to rape her and Joseph was thrown into prison, where he spent the next thirteen years. Once again his administrative skills were put to use, and he gained favor with the officials.

What went on in Joseph's mind? He was determined to be faithful to God and to a righteous way of life, but during the long, lonely nights, he must have wondered how his brothers and the others could do such things to him. Did he finally understand that his bragging had provoked the trouble?

Then came the dreams again—not Joseph's this time, but the dreams of two fellow prisoners. God gave him the gift of interpreting their dreams accurately and describing their outcome. Later, Pharaoh had a dream Joseph interpreted, a dream predicting years of prosperity followed by years of famine.

Joseph exalted

In Joseph, Pharaoh saw administrative qualities needed for the coming years of prosperity and famine. Joseph became second-in-command in Egypt and married Asenath with whom he had two sons. After so many years of suffering, Joseph finally had a peaceful, happy life.

The years of prosperity passed, and Joseph wisely

stocked grain and other provisions. Then, just as he had predicted, the drought came and the land dried up and produced no food. Egypt began to live off its surplus; they had enough to survive and even to sell to travelers who made their way to Egypt to buy from them, including Joseph's brothers.

They did not recognize the brother they had not seen in perhaps thirty years. Joseph, however, recognized them.

He chose not to reveal himself and treated them a bit roughly, testing them to see if their hearts had changed. He addressed them in the Egyptian language through an interpreter but listened carefully to their Hebrew conversations with each other.

Joseph demanded that they bring Benjamin back to prove that they were speaking the truth and then listened to what they had to say to one another. Their conversation, recorded in Genesis 42:21, softened his heart: "Surely we are being punished because of our brother. We saw how distressed he was when he pleaded with us for his life, but we would not listen; that's why this distress has come upon us."

Joseph sent them home, keeping Simeon in custody while the rest went back to their father.

Finally their supplies ran out and they appeared in Egypt again. This time Joseph created a situation in which his brothers could be fully pardoned and empowered to forgive themselves.

Then Joseph said to his brothers, "Come close to me." When they had done so, he said, "I am your brother Joseph, the one you sold into Egypt! And now, do not be distressed and do not be angry with yourselves for selling me here, because it was to save lives that God sent me ahead of you. For two years now there has been famine in the land, and for the next five years there will not be plowing and reaping. But God sent me ahead of you to preserve for you a remnant on earth and to save your lives by a great deliverance" (Genesis 45:4–7).

God intended it for good!

We admire Joseph because he was talented, kept himself pure from the advances of Potiphar's wife, had spiritual perception beyond the norm, was a capable administrator and a man of integrity, *but he was not faultless!* In his early days, he was dreamy, ambitious, and arrogant.

He had to be taken down a notch or two, and he was. Joseph is the perfect example of the way God fulfills His word: "Humble yourselves, therefore, under God's mighty hand, that he may lift you up in due time" (1 Peter 5:6). As God prepared Joseph to save entire nations, including His chosen people and Joseph's own family, the young man who was too enamored with himself to be humble needed to be brought down so God could exalt him. His brothers were part of that process.

Joseph moved from pride to self-pity to shame to bitterness and then to humility and forgiveness. Joseph became the man God wanted him to be, the man who could be exalted and not glory in his exaltation.

God knows our hearts; we have only our suspicions

How well do you handle humiliation and loss of position, recognition, and significance? My greatest fear in the ministry has always been that I would somehow disqualify myself from fulfilling God's plan for my life. I have prayed many times to be disciplined and pruned rather than discarded.

A few years ago I began praying what I now call my default prayer: "Help me to make my heart entirely Yours." I did not plan to pray in this way; I just began doing it at a time when things around me were dramatically changing.

When the organization I worked with restructured and took me out of the decision-making process, it hurt! When the church I attended experienced sweeping changes—many of which were negative, in my estimation—I spoke out. Although others felt the way I did, they didn't speak up, and I felt I had to become their voice.

I often stood alone in opposition to changes. I made suggestions that did not gain acceptance. I thought that my fear of disqualification was about to be realized.

Dolly and I felt like outsiders looking in. I spent many sleepless nights mulling over all the things I would like to say to certain people and what I thought they would probably say to me. Most of it was better left unsaid. Finally I resigned from the elders' board and we began attending another church. It was a low time in my life.

Pruning and discipline

One Sunday morning we attended a Bible class led by my friend David. Seated in a circle, we were taking turns reading a passage from Bruce Wilkinson's book *Secrets of the Vine*, when we read,

....

The vine's ability to produce fruit increases each year, but without intensive pruning the plant weakens and its crop diminishes. Mature branches must be pruned hard to achieve maximum yields.[1]

....

Suddenly I knew what was happening with me. First, God was pruning things from my life so I could narrow my focus and concentrate only on things He had called and gifted me to do. Second, I realized that God was answering my prayer to make my heart totally His.

He was taking away the things that had become too important to me, and He was freeing me to love Him the way I wanted and needed to. Once I saw this and looked forward (by hope and by prayer) to bearing more fruit, I began to thank Him for the losses I had suffered and the lessons I had learned. This made it easier to forgive.

I then understood that when we sincerely pray for God to help us make our heart entirely His, He may work in ways that we do not expect or like. He may take away things that are too important—things that we have allowed to compete with Him for our affection and loyalty.

Today I can see it all clearly. I have a new perspective on the happenings and a new outlook on life. I no longer blame certain people for the changes. I have forgiven them and moved on. We are friends again, and I understand that God used them in my life. I do not say that they intended anything for evil, but I do know that God intended it for good in my life.

"Son, your sins are forgiven."

MARK 2:5

CHAPTER

6

A Forgiveness
We Can Live With

Forgiving those who injure us must be tremendously important (1) because God calls us to it, and (2) because it can be so hard to do! It may be doubly hard due to the wounds we suffer and the misconceptions we bring to the experience. If we think, for instance, that to forgive is simply to say, "All is forgiven and forgotten and things are as they were before," we are probably headed for some confusing and conflicting times.

We are complex human beings. Our memories are not easily erased. Our emotions are not immediately healed. They become inner battlefields. Some offenses seem too wrong. Some pain seems too deep.

How can we forget the unforgettable? How can we

forgive the unforgivable? How can we live with ourselves if we feel we have not forgiven as we know we should?

As you prepare to forgive consider these four things:

Blessings—Think of the peace and the freedom and the blessings you will enjoy once you commit to forgiving and making that forgiveness permanent. Ask yourself: Do I want to feel good again?

Consequences—Contemplate the consequences of *not* forgiving. How long do you wish to prolong the feelings of resentment, guilt, and worthlessness?

Empowerment—Know that if you accept the challenge of forgiving, you can pray and expect to be enabled by the Holy Spirit to be able to forgive.

Mercy—In the process of accepting God's forgiveness and extending mercy to offenders, learn to be merciful to yourself.

The pain and resentment we feel after suffering a betrayal or an aggression are normal. Most people live with a certain amount of it. What many people do not experience is the freedom the Lord Jesus Christ provides when they ask Him to forgive them and empower them to forgive others.

Many resources are available to help us understand the process. One of my favorite books on the subject is *Total Forgiveness* by R. T. Kendall. A master preacher and former pastor of Westminster Chapel in London,

Kendall combines his experience with theological and psychological research to offer us a powerful and instructive book.

Another excellent book is *Forgiving and Reconciling* by Everett L. Worthington Jr. Worthington was an experienced counselor who had written previous works about forgiveness. In this book, Worthington tells how he was forced to deal with his own reactions to the senseless and brutal murder of his mother by burglars.

My own research has not been nearly as extensive nor my counseling experience as broad as these two capable men, but I have studied forgiveness for several years and have written extensively on the topic.

Although we have never met, the three of us have had our theories put to the test to see if we were willing to practice what we preached. I once wrote, "Forgive completely, unconditionally, generously, verbally, volitionally, and constantly." Many times I've asked myself if I could offer the forgiveness I had written about—or if I even wanted to.

Steps to forgiveness

Most of the literature about forgiveness includes instructions that affirm the following helpful steps. These liberating truths restore spiritual and emotional health. Don't take them as a formula, but see them as lessons that have been distilled through the lives of people like you and me who have been hurt and have had to learn to forgive.

1. Don't brush off the offense. Unless it is a minor offense, don't minimize the wrong, the mistake, or the pain felt. Nor should we overlook, condone, or approve the wrong that has taken place. What's wrong is wrong. It is a mistake to shrug it off as though we are too tough or too mature to be affected by it. It is also wrong to suspect that we deserved it or it wouldn't have happened to us.

Obviously some small offenses can be shrugged off or taken in stride ("be patient, bearing with one another in love," says Ephesians 4:2). But if the offense has been injurious to us or to our loved ones, we're better off admitting, "Yes, that hurt," before moving on. Even if we are able to see how God can use the offense to increase our godliness, we should not make light of the pain it caused. "Total forgiveness is achieved only when we acknowledge what was done without any denial or covering up—and still refuse to make the offender pay for his crime," says Kendall.[1]

2. Put yourself in the offender's shoes. Some offenses are understandably too horrible to comprehend. In many cases, though, you can try to understand what prompted the person to do what he or she did. What motivated him or her to do as he or she did? We have all had moments when we were not at our best. We have said or done things in the heat of emotion and while under stress that we now regret. Those who wounded us may have been at such a moment in their lives. We expect people to take those things into consideration when judging us, so let's be compassionate and forgive them as we expect them to do. "So in everything, do to others what you would have them do to you" (Matthew 7:12).

3. Make the tough decision that, with God's help, you will forgive. This means choosing not to retaliate, hate, reject, or get even with the person who hurt us. It also means that we are not going to speak or even think negatively about the person. It means not using the person's offense as an excuse for our own attitudes of self-pity or acts of wrongdoing. It means giving up resentment. Resentment means to "feel again" the pain and disappointment of the offense. Too often we rethink, relive, and resent the happenings that took place. To forgive is to obey God and follow as closely as we can the example and standard laid down for us by our Savior, Jesus Christ. As long as we hold onto a grudge, we are allowing that person's actions to continue hurting us. Someone once said, "Holding a grudge is like taking poison and waiting for the other person to die"!

4. Tell someone about it. It's difficult to be objective when our emotions are part of the equation. Bringing a person into the picture helps us recover that objectivity and sense of commitment.

When I was betrayed by a person I thought was a friend, telling someone—just one person—would have helped me to clarify my thoughts and commit myself to follow through. I don't mean telling someone what the person did (I have never done that and never will), but telling someone that the person hurt me and that I was committed to forgive. It would have helped me know that someone cared and was praying for me. Then when "the accuser of our brothers," as Satan is called in Revelation 12:10, suggested that I hadn't truly forgiven, I could have said, "Just ask my friend if I have forgiven. He'll tell you that I did!"

When I first went to Brazil, I did not see eye to eye with a colleague, and we had several clashes. I have since learned that it's best to talk through disagreements but to limit the discussion to the issue at hand. We should not attack the person's character but remain committed to the relationship. In those days I did not have the understanding or maturity for that. My colleague and I apologized to each other many times for our clashes.

Years went by, he moved away, and I rarely saw him. One day while traveling with a mutual friend, I commented that I was happy that the colleague and I had patched things up and there was no longer a problem between us.

This mutual friend was surprised and said, "He doesn't see it that way. He thinks you still owe him an apology."

I was shocked. I searched my memory for any incident that I hadn't straightened out. I could think of no unturned ground. Later I asked for the Holy Spirit's guidance and came to the conclusion that the problem was not due to a specific incident but to the painful accumulation of offenses. I had never acknowledged to him how deeply I had hurt him and how radically his life had been affected.

I sent off a letter detailing both of these issues and within a few days received an answer. I could tell that things had changed with him. He was not only receptive, but he also said that he was thankful and I was totally forgiven. It helped both of us put everything to rest, get on with our lives, and enjoy a newfound freedom. We are now close friends. Our mutual friend did us both a service.

5. Follow through. There is an act of forgiveness which may or may not be communicated to the offender, depending on the person's awareness of the offense. Then there is the process that follows.

In one case, I forgave a person for something offensive, but I was in a setting where the subject came up frequently. Each time it did, I had to reaffirm the forgiveness I had offered. Jokingly I remarked, "Jesus said, 'Seventy times seven.' That makes 490. Right now I'm at 483!" Quite honestly, I voiced that forgiveness so many times that every time I heard the person's name,

I would automatically declare, "He's forgiven!" He remains forgiven.

Once we are sure we have taken the first step of forgiveness, we embark on a commitment not to relive the offense or resent the offender. It is easy to slip. We think we deserve the right to feel sorry for ourselves, but once we turn down that road of self-pity, we need to do an immediate U-turn and change our thinking.

In his book, *Total Forgiveness*, R. T. Kendall gives a list of steps to forgiveness:[2]

1. Stop excusing, pardoning, or rationalizing.
2. Pinpoint the actions that have hurt you.
3. Spend time thinking of ways in which your life would be more satisfying if you could ever let go of your grievances.
4. Try replacing angry thoughts about the "badness" of the perpetrator with thoughts about how the offender is also a human being who is vulnerable to harm.
5. Identify with the offender's probable state of mind at the time of the occurrence. Understand the perpetrator's history while NOT condoning his or her actions.
6. Spend some time developing greater compassion towards the perpetrator.
7. Become more aware that you have needed other people's forgiveness in the past.

8. Make a heartfelt resolution not to pass on your own pain.
9. Spend time appreciating the sense of purpose and direction that come after steps one through eight.
10. Enjoy the sense of emotional relief that comes when the burden of a grudge has melted away. Enjoy also the feeling of goodwill and mercy you have shown.

Perhaps there is a name that affects you negatively. Maybe when you close your eyes you can see the face of an individual who has hurt you. Let me urge you to forgive and forgive and forgive again. Do not let the remembrance of their wrongdoing hurt you anymore. Do not allow yourself thoughts or words that leave you feeling guilty in regard to that person. Let go of the pain. Trust God for the grace to change your thoughts, words, and actions, and be free!

Bear with each other and forgive whatever grievances you may have against one another.

COLOSSIANS 3:13

It Can Get Complicated

I struggled to follow the agonizing narration of Rhee, a Korean immigrant to Brazil, who appeared at my office one day. He spoke broken Portuguese with a strong accent, making communication difficult. I strained to get the details.

Rhee had come to Brazil to make a fortune, leaving his wife behind with the promise, "I'll send for you when I can." He never imagined that life would be so difficult in the city of São Paulo. Since he had no savings, he could not take time out to study the Portuguese language. With no friends to open doors for him, he worked at the most menial tasks, earning just enough to stay alive. Seven years went by before he had saved enough to send a ticket to his wife.

Back in Korea, Rhee's wife grew tired of waiting and began to see other men. By the time she arrived in Brazil, she was not the woman he had left behind. She was angry and resentful, and she no longer loved him. She soon became interested in another man—and possibly more than one.

One day Rhee confronted the man she was seeing, and they fought violently. Rhee beat his adversary to death and was imprisoned for his crime. Some people escape from prison, and others escape to prison. That was the case with Rhee. Confined in São Paulo's "House of Detention," he heard the Christian gospel and surrendered his life to Jesus. He experienced forgiveness, and hope came to his heart. A weekly Christian group ministered to Rhee, and for the first time in many years he began to experience joy. Prison was a good experience for him, and he grew in the Lord.

When he was released, things changed. Back on the streets, he saw other Koreans prospering, but he remained poor and isolated. He tried to reconcile with his wife, but she wanted nothing to do with him. Left to himself, he became discouraged and bitter. Rhee convinced himself that his life had been destroyed by others and that the people who hurt him should in some way make retribution to him.

Finally a ministry attempted to help him rebuild his life. They gave him work to do and a place to live.

He submitted to the teachings and kept the rules, but he was not a happy man. Within the security of the Christian group he felt protected but dissatisfied and extremely restless.

I went to speak to the group, and a few days later, here he was at my doorstep—over 400 miles away. Was I his last hope? I hoped not. I could not blame him for feeling victimized, but in reality he was being victimized by himself, his foolish plans, his violent temper, and his bitter heart. The longer he pursued this reasoning, the more he would feel the victim.

Even the church he had attended wanted nothing more to do with him. There would be no restitution or reconciliation. The only things he could do were forgive those who had wronged him, put his unhappy past behind him, stand fast in the forgiveness he had received, and get on with his life. He was not prepared to do that.

Forgiven but unable to forgive

Few of us have such a tragic story to tell, but we all have a story. We have our heartaches, our regrets, and our bitter memories. We hold grudges. We seek revenge. Certain names, places, faces, and scenes produce negative reactions and remind us that we have problems to face and resolve. The person who is unable to forgive is often surprised by thoughts or feelings of anger, grief, and jealousy.

If we allow ourselves to dwell on thoughts like these, we run the risk of having a proverbial poisonous plant grow within us that will choke out our life and affect everyone around us. We must not let that parasitic plant take root. Hebrews 12:14–15 exhorts us: "Make every effort to live in peace with all men and to be holy; without holiness no one will see the Lord. See to it that no one misses the grace of God and that no bitter root grows up to cause trouble and defile many."

God is telling us: Live in peace, be holy, don't miss out on My grace, don't allow bitterness to grow, don't spread trouble, and don't defile others.

All around us, we see people who have lost their innocence and joy and have become bitter, unhappy individuals—but there is hope for them and for all of us.

He's with me wherever I go!

A Christian came to my office to talk about his unhappy relationship with someone close to him. He was resentful toward him and unwilling to forgive him. He said he would prefer to never see the person again but confessed that he was completely dominated by the image of this person in his mind.

"He's with me wherever I go. When I go on a trip, he goes along. When I come home, he's waiting there for me. When I get up in the morning, he's the first person

I see. When I lie down at night and close my eyes, I see him in the dark."

He wanted to get rid of this individual, but, ironically, the only way he could do it would be to forgive him, cancel his debt, and let it go. Without that, he might never find spiritual and emotional freedom.

A wake-up affair

A man discovered that his wife was having an affair with a professor while taking a night course at the university. Though he knew he had not invested in their marriage, he still felt betrayed, hurt, and very jealous. Despite the deficiencies in their marriage, her affair woke him up and heightened his longing for her. As a result, he consulted a counselor to see if the marriage could be saved.

During one of his appointments, he confessed he hated the professor and admitted that he had even dreamed of killing him. Although he was a Christian and a deacon in his church, he kept thinking of ways he could carry out an act of revenge.

When he began to understand the effects of his anger, he chose to forgive the professor and direct charitable thoughts toward him and toward his own wife. He was finally able to become free from his desire for revenge and to entrust the whole situation to God's care.

In a short time, he felt God's powerful intervention restoring the marriage. After dealing with the suffering, the unfairness, the anger, and the sense of loss, he was ready to take his wife back and discover a new depth of relationship that he had not known before. Love and forgiveness had worked a miracle.

Unforgivable?

Forgiveness is a crucial part of any meaningful relationship. We are all human and do things that hurt other people—sometimes the people we love the most. We expect more from them. When we get hurt, we often react by lashing out at the person who hurt us. By forgiving, we are empowered to move on without anger or hostility. If we hold on to those things, we allow the act of aggression we have suffered to continue hurting us.

What is an unforgivable act? A rape? A murder? A betrayal? A kidnapping? A child molestation? Perhaps we should say that some acts are too difficult for *immediate* forgiveness. Our first reaction may combine so much shock, pain, and anger that we are not able to forgive. If we allow ourselves time to process the information and the pain, we can eventually get to the place where forgiveness is possible. We should take as much time as we need to work through our feelings.

Choosing to forgive the perpetrator does not mean that we condone the act, nor does it mean that we should remain passive or in a situation where the person can hurt us again. We may forgive the person and still approve of his incarceration. The purpose is not only to punish the crime, but to protect society. Whatever the extenuating circumstances, one fact remains: We must forgive!

No unreasonable demands

Do not place unreasonable demands upon yourself in the process of forgiving.

Do not think you must feel good about the situation. You may never feel good about what happened, but you may begin to feel good about your forgiving response to it and about God's enabling grace.

Do not feel obligated to deepen a relationship with the person who hurt you. In some cases it is advisable; in other cases it is not. You should not place yourself in harm's way. Jesus rebuked some people and sent them on their way without any attempt to reconnect with them.

Do not try to do it on your own. Ask for and depend upon God's help to continue making the right choices and to receive the healing of your damaged emotions. Enlist the help of a trusted friend or counselor to help you understand what's going on internally and to hold you to your commitment to forgive.

Do not use the past offense as leverage over the perpetrator. The knowledge of a person's wrongdoing should not be passed on to others or used to pressure the individual.

Do not be too hard on yourself. No matter what you have done or what has been done to you, you are a person of value. Accept yourself, not as perfect, but as a unique and valuable creature of God's design.

Do not stay down. Do not allow your trauma to keep you distressed. Get up, get forgiven, get free, and get going again.

Forgive as the Lord forgave you.

COLOSSIANS 3:13

CHAPTER

8

Make Forgiveness Work for You

Some of the most useful and widely circulated material about forgiveness comes from the life and ministry of Dutch author and speaker Corrie ten Boom. Known as a Holocaust survivor, her story was made famous by her book entitled *The Hiding Place*.

When the Nazis stretched their tentacles into Holland, the Jewish population was hunted down, hauled away to prison camps, and murdered..

The Ten Boom family of Haarlem, Holland, committed the "crime" against the Third Reich of hiding Jews in a secret place above the family watch shop in their home. Many lives were saved, but eventually the Nazis arrested the Ten Booms and incarcerated them in prison camps. The father died in one camp. Corrie and her sister Betsie were taken to another, the notorious women's camp at Ravensbrück, Germany, fifty miles north of Berlin. When the women were allowed to bathe, they had to walk naked single file to the building where the showers were located, all while under the scrutiny of a dozen male guards. As they walked or stood in line, they were subjected to insults and lecherous looks from the prison guards.

Betsie was very pretty and had a delicate and attractive figure that attracted the attention of the guards. The lust on their faces and in their eyes was obvious. For Corrie, it was a humiliating and traumatic experience that left deep wounds in her soul. Betsie was constantly reminding Corrie that they needed to forgive the guards. Betsie later died in prison.

Despite all that Corrie suffered, she remained faithful to God and made a decision to forgive the Nazis. She promised God that after the war she would go wherever He wanted and take words of comfort to those who had suffered. Inwardly, she hoped that He would never call her to Germany. But, of course, He did. Here she tells what happens when she went to speak to a sad and distraught group of German believers.

Love your enemy

"The solemn faces stared back at me, not quite daring

to believe. There were never questions after a talk in Germany in 1947. People stood up in silence, in silence collected their wraps, in silence left the room.

"And that's when I saw him, working his way forward against the others. One moment I saw the overcoat and brown hat; the next, a blue uniform and a visored cap with its skull and crossbones. It came back with a rush: the huge room with its harsh overhead lights; the pathetic pile of dresses and shoes in the center of the floor; the shame of walking naked past this man. I could see my sister's frail form ahead of me, ribs sharp beneath the parchment skin. Betsie, how thin you were!

"The place was Ravensbrück and the man who was making his way forward had been a guard—one of the most cruel guards.

"Now he was in front of me, hand thrust out: 'A fine message, Fraulein! How good it is to know that, as you say, all our sins are at the bottom of the sea!'

"And I, who had spoken so glibly about forgiveness, fumbled in my pocketbook rather than take that hand. He would not remember me, of course—how could he remember one prisoner among those thousands of women?

"But I remembered him and the leather crop swinging from his belt. I was face-to-face with one of my captors, and my blood seemed to freeze.

" 'You mentioned Ravensbrück in your talk,' he was

saying. 'I was a guard there.' No, he did not remember me.

"'But since that time,' he went on, 'I have become a Christian. I know that God has forgiven me for the cruel things I did there, but I would like to hear it from your lips as well. Fraulein,'—again the hand came out—'will you forgive me?'

"And I stood there—I whose sins had again and again to be forgiven and could not forgive. Betsie had died in that place—could he erase her slow, terrible death simply for the asking?

"It could not have been many seconds that he stood there—hand held out—but to me it seemed hours as I wrestled with the most difficult thing I had ever had to do.

"For I had to do it—I knew that. The message that God forgives has a prior condition: that we forgive those who have injured us. 'If you do not forgive men their trespasses,' Jesus says, 'neither will your Father in heaven forgive your trespasses.'

"I knew it not only as a commandment of God, but as a daily experience. Since the end of the war I had had a home in Holland for victims of Nazi brutality. Those who were able to forgive their former enemies were able also to return to the outside world and rebuild their lives, no matter what the physical scars. Those who nursed their bitterness remained invalids. It was as simple and as horrible as that.

"And still I stood there with the coldness clutching at my heart. But forgiveness is not an emotion—I knew that too. Forgiveness is an act of the will, and the will can function regardless of the temperature of the heart. 'Jesus, help me!' I prayed silently. 'I can lift my hand. I can do that much. You supply the feeling.'

"And so, woodenly, mechanically, I thrust my hand into the one stretched out to me. And as I did, an incredible thing took place. The current started in my shoulder, raced down my arm, sprang into our joined hands. And then this healing warmth seemed to flood my whole being, bringing tears to my eyes.

"'I forgive you, brother!' I cried. 'With all my heart.'

"For a long moment we grasped each other's hands, the former guard and the former prisoner. I had never known God's love so intensely as I did then. But even so, I realized it was not my love. I had tried and did not have the power. It was the power of the Holy Spirit as recorded in Romans 5:5: '…Because the love of God is shed abroad in our hearts by the Holy Ghost which is given to us'" (KJV)[1]

Moving on

The experience of forgiveness does not end with the decision. If we allow ourselves to dwell on the details of the act we have forgiven, we may experience the resentment again and relive the experience to such a degree that the memory becomes as painful as it was when we first felt the injury.

Along with the pain may come deep frustration. We may think, "I already made the decision to forgive, but I guess it didn't work." Or we may hear that accusing voice of Satan saying, "If you had really forgiven, you wouldn't be feeling all this resentment now."

Our emotions do not always align with our choices. We made the decision because it was the right thing to do, but we still feel hurt. It is my observation that if we hold firmly to our decision to forgive and don't allow ourselves to dwell on the details of what hurt us, the emotions will eventually subside and align with our decision. Corrie ten Boom writes,

....

Forgiveness is like letting go of a bell rope. If you have ever seen a country church with a bell in the steeple, you will remember that to get the bell ringing you have to tug awhile. Once it has begun to ring, you merely maintain the momentum. As long as you keep pulling, the bell keeps ringing. Forgiveness is letting go of the rope. It is just that simple. But when you do so, the bell keeps ringing. Momentum is still at work. However, if you keep your hands off the rope, the bell will begin to slow and eventually stop.[2]

....

The offense starts the inner bell ringing. Every time we think about it, we are taking the rope in our hands and pulling it, causing the bell to ring another time. Then we make a decision to forgive and let go of the bell, but the bell of emotions keeps ringing. Momentum is created. The habit is formed. Every time we hear the bell ring, we tug at the rope again and prolong the ringing.

Now is time to let go of the rope. Even though the bell keeps ringing, if we choose not to pull at the memory, the ringing will grow softer and softer until it rings no more.

If we refuse to dwell on it, we will find healing for our emotions and the pain will subside.

The Lord says, "Forget what happened before."

ISAIAH 43:18 NCV

CHAPTER

9

Can I Ever Forget?

"Well, now, you just need to forgive and forget!" Really? A common misconception is that to forget offenses can only mean to have them completely wiped from our memory.

Forgetting is not a choice we can make. Our memories, like our emotions, are involuntary responses. We may choose to remember by repeating and taking note of things, but we cannot choose to forget.

A more realistic view is that we can be so healed from our hurts that we can remember them without being haunted by them.

"Forgive and forget" is a terrific motto to live by—if we understand what it means. It does not mean to repress a memory. That would be comparable to disregarding a nagging infection. Denial of its presence does not prevent the spread of destruction. The infection must be treated, and the infected areas must be healed.

The Random House Dictionary suggests four definitions for the word *forget*: (1) to cease or fail to remember, (2) to neglect intentionally, (3) to overlook or disregard, and (4) to cease or omit to think of something.

To forget in the healthy biblical sense is to intentionally disregard it and choose not to dwell on the offense or bring up the subject again, or hold it against the offender.

Our loving heavenly Father does not want us to feel guilty about our inability to have spotless memories. We are not required to feel good about the offenses that have occurred. God is a God of truth, and He knows we must face the reality of our sufferings and then forgive. We may remember and still forgive, but if we free the offender, we ourselves are set free.

Selective memory

David composed a fascinating prayer about God's memory in Psalm 25:6–7. "LORD, remember your mercy and love that you have shown since long ago. Do not remember the sins and wrong things I did when I was young. But remember to love me always because you are good, LORD" (NCV).

David was not asking God to lose His memory but

to be selective with it—to remember mercy and love but to forget the sins of his youth.

I think David understood that to forget does not mean to have amnesia. Rather, it means choosing not to hold it against the offender. In this case, David knew his sins were still registered in God's memory, but he asked God not to bring them up again or hold them against him.

His prayer aligned with God's character because once we have asked God to forgive our sins, He does not bring them up again. It should be the same with us. We must decide not to call up undesirable memories to brood on them or feed the hurts they once caused us. Healing can actually enable us to reflect on the situations painlessly and draw valuable lessons from them.

When Paul said he practiced "forgetting what is behind" in Philippians 3:13, he wasn't talking about leaving his socks in hotel rooms, and I'm sure he wasn't describing a once-and-for-all occurrence. At least six times in the Bible, Paul said he had persecuted Christians. His memory hadn't been erased, but he had dealt with his past in the way that God prescribes. His statement is amazing:

....

All the other apostles are greater than I am. I am not even good enough to be called an apostle, because I persecuted the church of God. But God's grace has made me what I am, and his grace to me was not wasted. I worked harder than all the other apostles. (But it was not I really; it was God's grace that was with me) (1 Corinthians 15:9–10 NCV).

....

Paul remembered that persecution of Christians had been part of his life, but he knew that God's grace was greater than all his sin—grace that forgave him, grace that enabled him to be effective. "Where sin increased, grace increased all the more" (Romans 5:20).

Like computer data, our past has been entered into our memory. We may see it pop up on the directory of our mind, but we do not have to download the file for review.

Choosing not to remember

When God forgives and "forgets" our sins, it means that He will never bring them up against us. We should do with the sins of others exactly what God does with ours.

We have already mentioned the story of Joseph, one of history's most engaging stories of forgiveness. Thirty years later Joseph had his chance for revenge, but he did not take it. Instead, he forgave his brothers. When he finally revealed himself to his brothers, they feared for their lives. By then Joseph had gained understanding from the Lord and healing for his wounds. God enabled him to care for his brothers and treat them kindly. He hadn't forgotten what they had done, but he refused to hold it against them.

In the ashes

Let me refer once more to Corrie ten Boom. The following experience is taken from her book *Tramp for the Lord*.

I recall the time...when some Christian friends whom I loved and trusted did something which hurt me.... Many years later, after I had passed my eightieth birthday, an American friend came to visit me in Holland. As we sat in my little apartment in Baarn, he asked me about those people from long ago who had taken advantage of me.

"It is nothing," I said a little smugly. "It is all forgiven."

"By you, yes," he said. "But what about them? Have they accepted your forgiveness?"

"They say there is nothing to forgive! They deny it ever happened. No matter what they say, though, I can prove they were wrong." I went eagerly to my desk. "See, I have it in black and white! I saved all their letters and I can show you where..."

"Corrie!" My friend slipped his arm through mine and gently closed the drawer. "Aren't you the one whose sins are at the bottom of the sea? Yet are the sins of your friends etched in black and white?"

For an astonishing moment I could not find my voice. "Lord Jesus," I whispered at last, "who takes all my sins away, forgive me for preserving all these years the evidence against others! Give me the grace to burn all the black and whites as a sweet-smelling sacrifice to your glory."

I did not go to sleep that night until I had gone through my desk and pulled out those letters—curling now with age—and fed them all into my little coal-burning grate. As the flames leaped and glowed, so did my heart. "Forgive us our trespasses," Jesus taught us to pray, "as we forgive those who trespass against us." In the ashes of those letters I was seeing yet another facet of His mercy.[1]

Corrie took a fresh step of obedience that would help her to truly forgive and forget in the most biblical sense of the word.

Unfinished business

When our memory haunts us in the area of right or wrong, it's often because our conscience, prompted by the Holy Spirit, is reminding us of some error that we need to correct. It's only when we correct the error that the nagging voice is silenced and we find peace. If we have done everything we know to do and the feeling of condemnation persists, we may suspect that an evil spirit is accusing us in order to keep us discouraged.

In that case we can follow the Bible's counsel of James 4:6–8: "'God opposes the proud but gives grace to the humble.' Submit yourselves, then, to God. Resist the devil, and he will flee from you. Come near to God and he will come near to you."

The first time

One Christian had been tempted constantly in an area of his life and had fallen occasionally into sin. Each time, he confessed his sin to God and asked forgiveness.

When he experienced another failure in that area, he said, "There I've gone and done it again. I'm sorry, Lord. Will you forgive me one more time?"

The Lord said, "Oh, had you done that before?"

God doesn't say, for instance, "Let's see, now, that's thirteen times you've hollered at your kids this month; how long do you think I'm going to keep forgiving you?"

Though He knows everything we have done, He treats each sin as though it were happening for the first time.

A God of grace and mercy

At the core of who God is, we find a heart of compassion and mercy. His thoughts toward us are good. He longs to bless us and draw us into an increasingly satisfying relationship. He forgives, He forgets, He redeems, He transforms, and He blesses us.

....

The LORD is compassionate and gracious, slow to anger, abounding in love. He will not always accuse, nor will he harbor his anger forever; he does not treat us as our sins deserve or repay us according to our iniquities. For as high as the heavens are above the earth, so great is his love for those who fear him; as far as the east is from the west, so far has he removed our transgressions from us. As a father has compassion on his children, so the LORD has compassion on those who fear him…. From everlasting to everlasting the LORD's love is with those who fear him, and his righteousness with their children's children (Psalm 103:8–13, 17).

....

The prophet Micah says, "You will again have compassion on us; you will tread our sins underfoot and hurl all our iniquities into the depths of the sea" (Micah 7:19).

To that Dwight L. Moody adds this note: "God has cast our confessed sins into the depths of the sea, and He's even put a No FISHING sign over the spot."

I can't forget my sin.

PSALM 51:3 NCV

CHAPTER

10

Can I Forgive Myself?

"I can't forgive myself. Even if God has forgiven me (and I hope He has), I will never be able to forget what I did or forgive myself."

What does someone mean when he or she says

—I have too many regrets,

—I wish things could have been different,

—I can't believe I let myself do that,

—I caused too much suffering,

—I'm so embarrassed and ashamed,

—I haven't suffered enough for what did,

—I need to atone,

—I don't deserve to be happy?

Do we deserve forgiveness?

I was surprised one day to hear a friend pray, "Thank you,

Lord. You've been merciful to us, even though there have been times when we didn't deserve your mercy."

The moment wasn't right for a theological discussion, but I thought, *When has receiving mercy ever depended upon our deserving it?*

Let's start with the right supposition: As sinners (and we all are), none of us deserves forgiveness. If we deserved it, we wouldn't need it. Mercy comes to us because a merciful God never stops being merciful. God extends His mercy to undeserving people. God's merciful arms are always outstretched toward us.

Beyond that, forgiveness comes because God in His mercy provided His Son Jesus Christ to pay the debt of our sin. Our repentance and faith in Christ releases His forgiveness, which comes to us through Christ's worthiness—not our own. And it comes to us through Christ's suffering, not ours.

The reformer Martin Luther was appalled by the ways the priests of his time handled the sin and guilt of the people. To wealthy parishioners, priests sold special indulgences said to provide escape from punishment for individuals and their relatives—dead or alive. To the poor they prescribed "penance"—a practice that sometimes included beating oneself with a whip. This was meant to help sinners feel worthy of forgiveness (or perhaps to encourage them to come up with the money to buy indulgences).

The practice has been eliminated from the church, but it lives on in many of our hearts. We berate ourselves and put ourselves through mental and emotional punishment, hoping someday to feel worthy of forgiveness. Only after we have suffered enough do we feel it may be all right to enjoy life again. Or, maybe we think that we could never suffer enough.

What can wash away my sin?

No punishment we suffer—self-inflicted or otherwise—can wash away wrongdoing. Sin is more serious than that. Only Jesus' blood shed on Calvary's cross can cleanse away guilt. Only His blood can bring peace to the anguished heart.

If suffering, sacrifice, or religious duty could make atonement for our sin, the value of our Lord Jesus Christ and His vicarious death for us would be diminished. Our value would be greater than His. If our suffering and sacrifice could make us deserving of salvation, the Father would have to apologize to Jesus for sending Him to suffer for us.

The songwriter understood well when he wrote
What can wash away my sin? Nothing but the blood of Jesus.
What can make me whole again? Nothing but the blood of Jesus.
Oh! Precious is the flow that makes me white as snow;
No other fount I know, nothing but the blood of Jesus.[1]

The only way

On a flight from Slovenia to Kosovo, I noticed that a flight attendant wore a tiny gold cross on a delicate chain around her neck.

"Does that mean you are a Christian?" I asked as she served me.

She thought for a moment and answered, "Yes, I am a Christian, but I don't often go to church because I disagree with the many people there who say that Jesus is the 'only way.'" She moved quickly to another passenger and our conversation ended.

As she went about her work, I thought to myself, *If the cross means anything, it means that Jesus is the only way. Why would the Father send His beloved Son to die if there was another way by which we could be saved?*

God has no apologies to make and no regrets concerning the sacrificial death of His Son. He has no hidden resentment toward us for causing Christ's suffering. His thoughts toward us are thoughts of peace not evil (Jeremiah 29:11).

God wants us to be forgiven and free! He wants our happiness to be restored. He offers abundant life to all regardless of what we have done. Rather than maintain an attitude of self-hatred, rejection, worthlessness, and unforgiveness, we should say, "I know I am unworthy of forgiveness, but if Christ died to provide it for me, how can I be so ungrateful as to reject it? If He has fully forgiven me, why should I be so foolish as to not forgive myself?"

Why should we forgive ourselves?

R. T. Kendall has written another book on forgiveness I found equally illuminating: *How to Forgive Ourselves—Totally*.

Kendall explains what he means by totally forgiving ourselves: "It is accepting God's forgiveness of all our past sins and failures so completely that we equally let ourselves off the hook for our pasts as God Himself has done. It also means that since I must forgive others totally, I must equally forgive myself totally."

He explains that many people feel guilty at the thought of totally forgiving themselves. "The idea is this," he says, "What I have done is so horrible that I do not deserve to be set free from guilt. It would be irresponsible to forgive myself totally and not look back. I must pay for my failure. I must see that I get justice."[2]

She felt polluted and abnormal

I was speaking on the subject of self-acceptance in a Brazilian church composed mostly of young Christians. I based my talk on David's affirmation in Psalm 139:14: "I praise you because I am fearfully and wonderfully made; your works are wonderful, I know that full well."

I asked the young people to consider that each of

them was a unique character, created by God with gifts and abilities to fill a special role in life. I urged them to be thankful for the way God made them and to accept themselves as they were.

After the meeting, a young woman shook my hand at the door and asked, "What if we can't accept ourselves, but it's not because of the way God made us?"

I could tell that her problem was not with her looks. She was a good-looking girl with a pretty face and trim figure. In fact, I could see that she was prettier than she allowed herself to appear. She preferred the tomboy look and seemed to be hiding her best attributes.

I asked, "Would you like to be more specific?"

She cowered a bit and said, "Mercy, no!"

"Would you like to talk?" I inquired.

"No," she said rather hesitantly and walked outside.

I noticed that she didn't leave but sat down in front of the church on the curb. When almost everyone was gone, I went over and asked, "Are you sure you wouldn't like to talk?"

Reluctantly she said she would.

She said she had weird dreams that many times were sexual in nature, and she considered them perverted. She thought there must be something wrong with her to have those kinds of dreams. She felt polluted and abnormal.

She began weeping and finally admitted, "I consented to have sex with my three brothers." Her emotional intensity suggested that these were recent events.

"When did this happen?" I asked.

"Let's see," she said, "I'm twenty-one now, and it happened when I was twelve."

"And it's never happened again?" I inquired.

"Never again!" she insisted.

"Not with anyone?"

"No! I'm a Christian now and I would never do that. Besides, I think I'm a little abnormal!"

I insisted that she wasn't abnormal. "You've behaved properly for nine years. You are a normal person who has been hurt, and you have some deep scars that keep reappearing."

When I assured her that she was normal, she began to weep again. Could she allow herself to believe that?

I asked her to do the difficult thing she had never had the courage to do before—to talk with her three brothers and ask for their forgiveness. (In reality, they should have asked her, but I had no access to them and she had been a consenting partner.)

She went home determined to set things straight but almost lost courage. Finally she went to her brothers one by one and said, "You remember what we did when we were younger? Please forgive me." Each of them responded in the same fashion: "Thank you for bringing it up, and please forgive me, too."

Having been forgiven by God and by her brothers, she was able to forgive herself and allow herself to be feminine again. Her lovely features reappeared, and the change was enormous.

The purest of virgins

Sexual sins always seem to be cloaked in a special kind of shame—especially for women. Though God doesn't appear to see these acts—perverted as they may be—as worse than other sins, they have a way of leaving a mark upon us. Many women find it especially difficult to regain their sense of worth after involvement in sexually immoral behavior.

Several years ago I spoke to the students of a Bible institute. During the sermon, I felt prompted to switch topics for a moment and say, "If there is a young girl here who has fallen into the sin of fornication but has repented of that sin, I want you to know that God sees you as the purest of virgins."

Later that day a young woman said, "Thank you, Pastor. Those words were for me. You'll never know how much they meant."

Go and sin no more

A woman was dragged into the presence of Jesus to be judged for her sin of adultery. The mob reminded Jesus that Moses determined such women should be stoned.

"Now what do you say?" they asked.

Jesus said to the mob, "If any one of you is without sin, let him be the first to throw a stone at her."

After they had left, Jesus turned to the woman and said, "Woman, where are they? Has no one condemned you?" She responded, "No one, sir." Jesus then looked at her and spoke words that have been repeated for centuries around the world: "Then neither do I condemn you…. Go now and leave your life of sin" (John 8:5–11).

Something tells me the strength the woman received at that moment enabled her to leave her past behind and live a transformed life from then on. That's what Jesus wants for all of us.

Great sin, greater love

Another woman with a similar story felt such gratitude and love to Jesus for His forgiveness that she washed His feet with tears and perfume and wiped them dry with her hair.

The self-righteous Pharisees, who admitted no need (and perhaps no provision) for forgiveness, criticized the woman's extravagant act. And they scorned her for her sinful past.

Jesus understood her perfectly and accepted her love. He turned to Simon, his disciple, and said, "'Two people owed money to the same banker. One owed five hundred coins and the other owed fifty. They had no money to pay what they owed, but the banker told both of them they did not have to pay him. Which person will love the banker more?' Simon, the Pharisee, answered, 'I think it would be the one who owed him the most money.' Jesus said to Simon, 'You are right'…. Jesus said to the woman, 'Because you believed, you are saved from your sins. Go in peace." (Luke 7:41–43, 50 NCV). Part of the difficulty with forgiving ourselves is that we have to identify what we have done and take responsibility for it. When we do that our offense becomes part of our reputation.

A young woman was sentenced to five years in prison. After having had sex with a partner who then wanted nothing more to do with her, she obtained the help of a friend, tied the man up, and used a hot metal object to brand the letter *R* onto his abdomen, leaving a permanent scar. Her lawyer said, "She's a good kid—despite the picture painted of her—who exercised poor judgment and got herself into a bad situation. She is not the monster the prosecution made her out to be."

One political candidate had been a comedian and a writer. It was discovered that he had written an article in extremely bad taste for *Playboy Magazine*. His party officials excused his behavior saying, "That was the comedian; this is the politician." Were they two different people? It's possible that he has repented, but I certainly wasn't convinced by the argument given by the party member. Was it excusable for the comedian but not the candidate? Were they not one and the same?

What we do is the result of the kind of people we are. We commit sins because we are sinful at heart. Taking ownership of sin means we suffer consequences.

Give me joy!

Should a Christian who has committed a terrible sin ever allow himself the luxurious feeling of joy? When King David was faced with the double sins of adultery and murder, he prayed, "I know about my wrongs, and I can't forget my sin. You are the only one I have sinned against; I have done what you say is wrong. You are right when you speak and fair when you judge" (Psalm 51:3–4 NCV).

Once David had repented of his sin and accepted God's forgiveness, he did not think it was too much to ask, "Restore to me the joy of your salvation and grant me a willing spirit, to sustain me" (Psalm 51:12). Read Psalm 32:1 and you understand how fully God answered David's prayer: "Happy is the person whose sins are forgiven, whose wrongs are pardoned" (NCV).

Before his conversion, the apostle Paul was known as Saul, persecutor of the Christian church. When Stephen became the first Christian martyr, stoned to death for his dedication to and defense of the gospel, Saul stood and watched.

Paul could have been guilt-ridden for the rest of

his days. Instead, he lived by the words that he leaves as counsel for you and me in Philippians 3:13–14: "But one thing I do: Forgetting what is behind and straining toward what is ahead, I press on toward the goal to win the prize for which God has called me heavenward in Christ Jesus."

Where can we unload our guilt?

David Seamands once pointed out in a sermon that there are only three places we can deposit the guilt of our sins:

1. On the cross, where Jesus "carried our sins in his body...and [we] are healed because of his wounds" (1 Peter 2:24 NCV).
2. On ourselves, where through self-inflicted suffering and emotion-based sickness we try to make atonement for our wrongdoings.
3. On others, usually the people closest to us, who bear the marks of our anger and frustration by becoming scapegoats for everything wrong that happens to us.[3]

The right place is obviously the cross. Should we forgive ourselves? Should we allow ourselves to feel fully forgiven? I suggest that

- if forgiveness stems from God's merciful character... (and it does!)
- if is forgiveness is available to us through Christ's atonement... (and it is!)
- if God no longer considers us guilty... (and He doesn't!)
- if God no longer remembers our sins against us... (and He doesn't!)
- if God is worthy of our trust... (He is infinitely worthy!)

then, though we are less worthy than we can possibly imagine, we should consider ourselves truly forgiven—not through our worthiness, but His. Not by our suffering, but His. Not by what we can pay, but by what He has paid. If He can forgive us, then for His sake, for our sake, for everyone's sake, let us forgive ourselves.

"I do believe! Help me to believe more!"

MARK 9:24 NCV

CHAPTER

11

Forgiving by Faith

Sometime we may feel unable to forgive. Forgiveness then demands a power that is greater than our own. By being willing to forgive, we have already taken the first step—but we need God's help to forgive freely and fully.

Help is available to all who ask for it and receive it by faith. Trusting in the power of the Spirit who indwells us and fills us, we can find the ability to love and forgive.

My good friend Caio tells a personal, moving story of that power. I have seen what a beautiful work of restoration God has done in his family. I translated this story from Portuguese.

Forgiveness at Christmastime

"She was pretty, there was no denying that. Blond, shapely, provocative, extroverted—she was a Brazilian Marilyn Monroe. She was my father's lover. I saw her for the first time when I was seven years old and vowed that one day I would kill her for what she was doing to my mother.

"As I remember it, Mama seemed to cry most of the time, first sharing her tears with her own mother and then with me. Though I was too young to understand, I could feel all the hurt and humiliation that were now part of her life.

"At home, in the Amazon River city of Manaus, my father and mother went days, weeks, even months without exchanging a word. I became their messenger, asking for money and delivering it, carrying notes, becoming their voice to one another to communicate only the most essential information, nothing more. The more my mother cried, the more cynical my father became.

"Then one day, Mama—although she probably knew she would lose control of her emotions—packed me in the car and took me to visit this woman who had caused us so much pain. I suppose she thought that by taking me, a little boy, along she could convince her rival to leave my father alone. But our visit ended in humiliation when we found the woman in my father's arms. We had no choice but to return home. How I hated that woman for ruining our lives!

"I was already insecure, but things got worse for our family. Dad lost 80 percent of everything he had, and we were forced to move from Manaus to Rio de Janeiro. Dad carried a gun, determined to kill a group of eight men before they could kill him. Every day, I expected to see him carried home in a casket.

"Eventually we moved across the bay to Niteroi, where Dad had a transforming experience with Jesus Christ. At the same time, the grace of Christ met Mom in a new way. Later we moved back to Manaus, where Dad became a minister.

"Although I rebelled for a few years and refused to have anything to do with my parents' faith, Christ eventually brought change into my life, as well. Our family was united in faith and love. At the age of twenty-one, I, too, completed the required studies and was ordained a minister, to serve alongside my father in a large church.

"One day, as I was going to make a pastoral call, I thought of my father's former companion. In my memory she was still beautiful, but how would she be in real life? Was she happy? Had she found another companion? What was she like now?

"I drove by the beauty parlor she owned. Then, looking toward the shop, I heard an inner voice say, 'Go in and see her.'

"I couldn't believe what I was hearing and feeling. The wound was reopened in my soul, and I struggled, saying, 'God, don't you know I was just going to drive by this place? Couldn't you find someone else to share the gospel with this woman?' But the conviction wouldn't go away: 'Go in and talk to her. Treat her as if she were your own mother.'

"Reluctantly, I stopped the car to pray. Tears came to my eyes as I resisted the impulse of God's Spirit. Finally I said, 'All right, Lord, I'll go.' I got out and, standing at the door of the salon, I could see her across the room.

"She was still pretty, about fifty, I thought, but very attractive.

"She looked up and recognized me at once. 'You're Dr. Caio's son, aren't you?'

"'Yes, ma'am, I am.'

"'You're the preacher on the TV show. I've been watching you.'

"'Yes.'

"'You must hate me,' she said.

"'No, much to the contrary. I've come here to tell you that I love you and I want to respect you like I do my own mother.'

"Hearing those words, she began to weep and, as I saw her tears, my eyes filled, too. Clinging to me, she led the way to a small room behind the salon where she confessed, 'I'm a disgrace. I've spent my whole life ruining marriages, destroying families—not just yours—there are others. My life is a hell. I'm all alone. No one wants me. No one respects me.'

"I listened to her and felt pity. When she had finished talking, I excused myself and went straight to my parents' home. I asked Mama and Dad if we could go into their bedroom to talk. There in the quietness of their most intimate setting, we talked about how God had come into our lives and changed the direction of our family. They both rejoiced with me as we all remembered what God had done.

"'But,' I said, 'what about that woman? We're happy, but she's not. Is she going to have to remain in her miserable spiritual condition forever?'

"My mother interrupted me. 'No! I pray for her every day. I want her to be saved.'

"'Then you ought to share the gospel with her,' I said too quickly.

"Mama answered immediately. 'Oh, son, I pray that God will use someone else, because it's too hard for me. She robbed me of my very life. She took years away from me. I have no hatred toward her, but I can't love her like I know I should. That's why I ask Jesus to send someone else.'

"'Well then,' I answered, 'God has already answered your prayers, because I went to see her. I told her I want to love her like I love you. She says she would like to see you but is too ashamed. I invited her to church, but out of respect for you, she says she will not come.'

"Mama was not prepared for that. She answered, 'That's asking too much of me. I can't do it.'

"Disappointed, I said nothing more but began visiting my new friend regularly. I read the Bible and prayed with her almost daily for nearly two months.

"Christmas was always special at our house, because it was just one week before that wonderful celebration that Dad had given his heart to the Lord. Now it was Christmas Eve and the whole family was gathered together—brothers, sisters, wives, children, Mama and Dad.

"I knew that the Holy Spirit had been speaking to Mama, and I thought she might be ready to face her former adversary. 'Mom,' I asked, 'could we all join together as a family choir and go over to her house to sing for her?'

"Mama hesitated, but her resistance was gone. 'Yes, yes,' I heard her agree. 'We can go.' With her consent, we practiced three hymns and drove to the woman's house.

"It was dark when we arrived there, so we stopped outside the gate and began to sing. As our voices reached up to her window, it opened just a crack. I could see her shadow. She was watching and listening.

"Then the light came on. Soon she was at the door. Her face was bathed in the softly glowing light. Mom took a step toward her, a step of faith and obedience.

Then the woman who had hurt Mom so deeply took a step toward her, and suddenly, somewhere between the gate and the door, they embraced with tears running down their faces.

"We kept singing of the Prince of Peace while they hugged and kissed and washed away their pain in the tears of forgiveness.

"Then it was Dad's turn. No one objected when he hugged her. It wasn't the hug of a lover; it was the hug of a friend.

"And they are still friends. *We* are still friends—Mama, Dad, me, my whole family, and the woman I had wanted to kill. We love each other and care for each other as true friends should."[1]

Trust God to make forgiveness work. Even if the person does not respond, you will gain a victory for doing your part.

"As the father has sent me, I now send you....
If you forgive anyone his sins,
they are forgiven; if you do not forgive them,
are not forgiven."

JOHN 20:21, 23

CHAPTER

12

Who to Forgive

Everyone needs to be forgiven and to forgive. Christ wants to use us to take forgiveness to the world. Where do we start? Perhaps we should start by forgiving God. "Wait a minute!" you object. "God has done no wrong and has made no mistakes. God does not need our forgiveness!" I agree, but for our sakes we may need to forgive Him. Although in our minds we accept that God is absolutely righteous, loving, just, and merciful— in our hearts we may hold conscious or unconscious grudges toward Him for the way He has made us or for things He has allowed to happen.

We read Romans 8:28—"And we know that in all things God works for the good of those who love him, who have been called according to his purpose"—and we wonder what's gone wrong.

What's good about this? Haven't I been called? What's His purpose?

The truth is, His purpose is higher than ours and we don't understand it. Sometimes hard times are required for us to decide to rise to His purpose, which is to be "predestined to be conformed to the likeness of his Son" (Romans 8:29).

God works in us to make us more like Christ—patient, holy, and surrendered to His will. The difficulties we face become the tools He uses to achieve His purpose. The sooner we understand that and surrender our lives to His leading, the sooner our purpose will align with His purpose and He will have freedom to do what will be for our highest good.

To prevent all suffering, God would have to abandon His highest purpose or violate our free will or the free will of others who intentionally or unintentionally hurt people. None of us wants to be a marionette with God pulling every string. We cherish the ability to choose our actions. To have that freedom, we must also be willing to live with the consequences of our freedom and the freedoms of others.

That freedom results in several kinds of suffering:
—we make wrong choices and suffer as a

result of them;

— we make wrong choices, and others suffer as a result of them;

— other people make wrong choices and suffer because of them;

— other people make wrong choices, and we suffer because of them;

— we suffer and others suffer for unexplainable reasons.

Who's responsible for what?

After a solitary dinner in a Santiago, Chile, hotel, I talked with a waiter who said, "I cannot believe in a God of love."

I asked him what had happened to destroy his faith.

"Last Monday night," he said, "I went at 11:00 p.m. to catch my bus home from work. At the bus stop, I found a person stretched out under a bench, trying to sleep. My first reaction was, *A God of love wouldn't let that happen, therefore, there is no God of love.* As the week went by, I saw that person each night and my anger grew steadily. Friday night it came to a boil when I discovered the person was a woman. A God of love would not allow that to happen to a woman."

I thought to myself, *How interesting. Five nights in a row he sees that woman lying there but does nothing to help. When he finally does react, it's just to raise his fist and blame God.*

Friends, something is wrong with our thinking. So often when we say, "God, why don't you *do* something?" God is saying, "And why don't *you* do something?"

God, I believe, was grieved more deeply about the woman's situation then the waiter was and is grieved simultaneously by millions of situations more painful than anything the waiter had ever seen or imagined.

One thing that grieves God is that He has entrusted His work to us, His people, and we fail to identify or carry out our responsibilities. The guilt is not God's; it is ours!

Although we should respond to human need, God knows why that woman was under the bench. It's possible that in her journey toward the Lord or her flight from Him, that was the best place she could possibly be.

Why do we hold grudges against God? Often it's because we are resisting Him or do not understand what God is really like. Subconsciously we superimpose the face of another authority figure upon God's face: "I might have known; God is just like my dad (or my teacher or my coach or my boss)!"

Maybe "forgiving God" isn't the best way to say it, but we need to clear Him of whatever charges we hold against Him and offer Him the love He deserves. We need to stop standing in judgment of Him. We need to correct our thinking and seek to know Him better. We need to rid ourselves of grudges that we have held against Him.

Forgiving parents

My father's story is a sad one. His own father was hard on him, so he ran away from home at the age of fifteen, stole a car, and drove it across the state line into Iowa, where he was arrested. Not wanting to be sent home and having no documents, he lied about his age, stating that he was eighteen. He was placed in an adult prison where he often proved to be incorrigible. That resulted in a prolonged sentence, and he was released seven years later.

After he married, he vowed that none of his sons would spend time behind bars. That, of course, was a correct desire, but his way of preventing our imprisonment was wrong. He turned our home into a prison! All five of us brothers—George, Doug, Burt, Bart, and Ken (in order of age)—had to forgive Dad and deal with personal traumas related to him. Here's what we have to say about forgiveness.

George (me)—"When I was sixteen, I was as angry with Dad as he had been with his father. One cold Saturday night I caught a ride with a trucker headed for South Dakota. As I rode down the highway toward what I imagined to be freedom from his overbearing ways, I thought about three things: What would I do with my life? What would happen if Dad caught up with me? How could I put Mom through so much suffering?

"I came to my senses and went to my maternal grandparents' home. The next day they took me to church, and I heard the sermon of the prodigal son (see Luke 15:11–32). Grandpa negotiated a peaceful return home for me, and Dad became a bit more permissive. We tried harder to communicate with each other.

"I forgave Dad but always dreaded the excessively dramatic occasions when we would be together. When Dolly and I were leaving for Brazil as missionaries, Dad shook my hand and said he knew he would never see me again. He was right. Less than four months later, he was killed in an accident. My pain and bitterness were gone by then. I was sorry to hear that he had died and hoped that he had made his peace with God, but I never really missed him or mourned for him."

Doug—"Did I forgive him? Yes! I did share my testimony with him, but I don't remember him saying anything afterward. I tried to show him forgiveness by going to his apartment; repairing, tuning, and putting brakes on his car; and listening patiently to his loud pipe-organ music. If I had told him that I forgave him, he would have had to admit that he did something wrong, and that wasn't going to happen. I prayed for him a lot.

"About a year before Dad was killed, I talked to Rev. Griffith, our former pastor, and told him that I had never heard Dad say one good thing about me in his life. That was when I learned Dad bragged about all of us to him. I know Dad had problems, and I don't harbor anything against him."

Burt—"When I was just a little boy, Dad would hit me and I would go flying across the room. After I was in an automobile accident, Dad changed his tactics. Instead of hitting me, he used verbal abuse: 'You'll never amount to a hill of beans. All your brains leaked out through the hole in your head.' Growing up, I tried to stay clear of him and not be noticed.

"Memories of the abuse haunted me for fifty-five years, and when I talked about it with friends, they suggested that I drive from my home in Minneapolis to his gravesite in North Dakota and say what I had to say. Forty years from the day of his death, I got in my car and drove to his gravesite. I returned some of the verbal abuse that he had given me. I told him I *did* amount to something. Finally I spat on his grave, closed the car door, and drove away. About halfway between Jamestown and Valley City, North Dakota, God's Spirit spoke to me: 'You forgot something.' I knew immediately what it was, and I finally said the most important words of the 700-mile trip— 'I forgive you!' "

Bart—"I hated Dad for the humiliation and outbursts of violence that occurred. I used to pray that something would happen to him. An accident was the preferable means in my eight- or nine-year-old mind.

"Later, after becoming a Christian, I started praying for the members of our family. Eventually I prayed for Dad. I tried to tell him that I had asked Jesus to be my Savior, but he never let me dwell on the subject.

"When I was eighteen years old, I was teaching Vacation Bible School. The missionary called me out of class and told me that Dad had been killed in an auto accident the day before. After hearing the news, I walked for a while, finally arrived at home, threw myself on the bed, and wept for a long time. I had never told Dad that I forgave him.

"After that I was like a walking time bomb. Every now and then, there would be a minor explosion and I would have to apologize to someone. A psychologist asked me about Dad, and I realized that—though I had volitionally forgiven him (out of Christian duty)—I still harbored resentment inside of me. The psychologist helped me get rid of a lot of pent-up violence.

"I also learned to forgive. One evening when our daughter Sharon was nine, she was not quite sassy but very indifferent toward me. I took her into the next room and asked her if she thought maybe she had been a little hard on her daddy. I waited for her to make things right, but she said, 'No, I don't think so.' I waited a little longer and finally said, 'I guess you might as well go to bed then.'

"Walking her to the stairs, I watched her go up to her room. I waited at the foot of the stairs for about ten minutes, thinking she would come down, throw her arms around my neck, and say she was sorry. It was a long ten minutes, and I finally realized she wasn't coming. Before I walked away, though, I felt that God was saying to me, 'I know...' And I could visualize God waiting at the stairs for me and for 5 billion other people to come back and say 'I'm sorry.' He didn't wait with a raised fist, as some people imagine, but with open arms. He would take them all unconditionally, the way I would with Sharon."

Ken—"My mode to deal with Dad was silence. In fact, I didn't speak to anyone I didn't trust, so my brothers and my mother knew my voice, but very few others ever heard me speak a word until I was in the third grade. I even made up words that only my family understood.

"Hospitalized with rheumatic fever at age five and then placed in a psychiatric hospital to discover the source of my emotional problems, I wasn't released until my father had left the home for good.

"I believe that forgiveness comes naturally to children. It takes years to learn that our power to forgive can be held back to inflict pain on the object of our unforgiveness. Having been convinced by many voices that I should hate and reject my father, I eventually gave in. He was the invisible object of my anger and scorn. It wasn't until long after he was gone that, on one particular occasion when I was subjected to loud organ music, a response was triggered in me that I didn't even know was there. For the first time I wept for my father, and I made a decision to forgive him and put that pain behind me. My hope is that he did have a saving knowledge of Christ."

It is not easy to forgive dysfunctional parents. They leave scars upon us, and we discover that the deeper the scars, the harder it is to forgive. But whatever it takes, it is worth the effort to bring healing between parents and children. The last promise of the Old Testament shows God's concern for reestablishing this relationship."

....

I will send you Elijah the prophet.... Elijah will help parents love their children and children love their parents (Malachi 4:5–6).

....

Brothers and sisters

The earliest families on record experienced serious conflicts between siblings. Cain was so jealous of Abel's faith and acceptance before God that he murdered him. Jacob took advantage of his twin brother Esau's hunger to rob him of his birthright. Later he deceived his father, Isaac, and cheated Esau out of the family blessing, as well. Then Jacob ran for his life. Jacob married first Leah and then Rachel, sisters who were bitterly jealous of each other. Jacob's sons sold his favorite son Joseph as a slave to Egypt. These were not happy families.

Hurtful words are spoken, and humiliating things happen between brothers and sisters that can result in lifelong grudges. Some resent having to live up to their older sibling's reputation—whether good or bad. Others feel that favoritism has been shown. Much long-standing resentment could be cleared up if brothers and sisters would open up with each other, talk things out, and forgive the hurts of the past.

My good friend Dick's mother died in childbirth. He was shuffled back and forth between home and an orphanage. Eventually, he was taken in by a brother and his young wife.

Dick's sister-in-law tried her best to help him, but she didn't know how to handle a small boy. She told him if he misbehaved, he would be thrown out of the home. "Then where will you go? Nobody wants you, you know." Birthdays were horrible for Dick. Each year someone reminded him that if it weren't for his birth, his mother would still be alive.

It was a wonderful day when Dick invited Christ into his life. He learned to feel at home in the family of God. Called to be a missionary, Dick attended a Bible college, where he learned to walk with God and correct the wrongs he had done in the past. Remembering the spiteful things he did to get even with his sister-in-law, Dick wrote a letter asking for her forgiveness. When she read the letter, she was so moved that she framed it and became extremely proud of Dick. Eventually Dick became a missionary and served as a valuable member of a Bible institute staff.

Dick encouraged many people when he shared his story. But he and his wife, Bernice, noticed that each time he told the story, he would weep painfully.

In 1977, Dick and Bernice attended a seminar and received prayer for healing of the memories. The leaders seemed to receive special insight from God. While praying with Dick, they were enabled by the Holy Spirit to cite specific moments in Dick's life when he had been hurt. They asked God to walk through the corridors of Dick's mind and heal every hurtful place.

Dick has never again been troubled by painful memories. He can now look back on those experiences with no heartache or bitterness. He has not forgotten the events but neither is he disturbed by any of them. Dick and Bernice have a happy marriage and two grown children who serve the Lord. To see Dick and his family together, you would never suspect that he had suffered so much as a child.

Spouses and former spouses

J. Allen Peterson, a well-known Christian marriage counselor, described a treatment used by a colleague when all other techniques failed.

A woman went to a counselor's office and said, "It's all over. I can't take it anymore. I want a divorce immediately."

In a last effort, the counselor asked, "Are you going to let him off that easy? You should make him suffer first before you send him away."

"How can I do that?" the lady asked.

"First, you have to convince him that you really love him. It will take you about a month, but here's what I want you to do. Go home and get into your best dress. Meet him at the door and tell him that you love him. Have his favorite dinner waiting for him. Try every day to do something special, and make him feel like a king. At the end of thirty days, tell him it was all a big act, that you can't stand him, and that you want a divorce."

Her desire for vengeance was so great that she decided to do it. Right away she began acting out the role of a loving wife. She literally spoiled her husband, doing everything she could to please him.

After thirty days, the counselor called to ask how things were going: "Do you still want to go through with the divorce?"

"Divorce?" she exclaimed. "I never wanted a divorce. My husband has been so kind for the past month that I could never think about leaving him. He's the sweetest man in the world!"

What happened? At first she had no feelings of love

and forgiveness, but she acted as though she did. Her husband warmed to her affection and began to fulfill her expectations. Gradually her feelings of affection returned, and she was able to fulfill his expectations, as well. They fell deeply in love.

Many times love and forgiveness need to be acted out as a choice of the will rather than fluttering emotions.

Forgiving a divorce

I can't believe that God requires a person to continue in a marriage if it means danger to one's physical well-being or if continual unfaithfulness destroys any possibility of reconciliation. Neither do I believe that an act of unfaithfulness is a call for automatic divorce. It is a call for confrontation, counseling, maybe temporary separation, but above all, a call for repentance, forgiveness, and reconciliation.

In today's culture, divorce has become common among Christians. Thank God, some churches have become effective in reaching those who have gone through the tragedy of divorce. Those who are divorced must find understanding and forgiveness in the church. But the church must never compromise on God's standards or fail to communicate His disapproval of this social tragedy and sin. Malachi spoke to the problem in strong words.

You cover the LORD's altar with tears. You cry and moan, because he does not accept your offerings and is not pleased with what you bring. You ask, "Why?" It is because the LORD sees how you treated the wife you married when you were young. You broke your promise to her, even though she was your partner and you had an agreement with her.... The LORD God of Israel says, "I hate divorce. And I hate people who do cruel things as easily as they put on clothes," says the LORD All-Powerful. So be careful. And do not break your trust. (Malachi 2:13–14, 16 NCV)

Since God takes our marriage vows seriously, we cannot pass over them lightly. "Until death do us part" is a pledge that eliminates the possibility of divorce except for the exceptions listed above. Neither divorce nor remarriage frees a person from the responsibility to forgive and seek forgiveness

Forgiveness between nations

Paraguay is a small South American nation with a population of 3 million bilingual people. Years ago Paraguay had become an advanced civilization. South America's first railroad was built in Paraguay. Their agriculture economy thrived. Laws were enforced, and crime was practically unknown.

But the thriving country was a threat to other nations, so Brazil, Argentina, and Uruguay banded together to fight against Paraguay. The War of the Triple Alliance resulted, killing more than 90 percent of Paraguay's adult males and enormous numbers of women and children. History tells of six-year-old boys bearing arms to defend their country and dying in battle. Pregnant women were shot in the womb. Large portions of Paraguay's land were seized by Brazil.

An important statue now stands between the Paraguayan national airport and the capital city of Asunción. It depicts a mother and her child standing beside a fallen husband. Paraguayans have never forgotten that war.

I talked about these historical facts with the young people—Brazilian, Paraguayan, and Argentinian—at a teaching session in Paraguay. I suggested that it would be wonderful to bring representatives of these people together for a moment of reconciliation.

Myriam, a young Argentinian girl who grew up in Paraguay, shared the idea with Christian leaders. They, in turn, called Paraguayan, Argentinian, Brazilian, and Uruguayan missionaries to a prayer encounter on one of the main plazas of Asunción. About 3,000 people watched the missionaries, each carrying the flag of his own offending nation, ask forgiveness of the Paraguayan people. Prayer was then offered for healing of relationships while Paraguayan believers stood in the plaza and wept. Forgiveness flowed between Christians of the four nations, and people reconsecrated their lives to the Lord.

A few months after this forgiveness encounter took place, I sat alongside a Paraguayan government official on a flight between major cities in Brazil. I told him that I loved Paraguay and knew what a terrible injustice had been committed against his nation. Then I told him how the Christians had gathered to ask for forgiveness. To my surprise, the official, with tears in his eyes, invited me to his home the next time I visited Paraguay.

Because Christ has made it possible for all barriers to be broken down, let us take the message of forgiveness and reconciliation to all the nations of the world for the sake of Christ and his kingdom and forgive everyone.

Speaking the truth in love, we will in all things grow up into him who is the Head, that is, Christ.

EPHESIANS 4:15

CHAPTER

13

Caring Enough to Risk Confrontation

How do you face the head of a nation with the double accusation of adultery and murder—if you value your own life? Many prayers must have gone up to God before the prophet Nathan appeared in David's throne room in 2 Samuel 12 to confront the king. Nathan told the story of a wealthy man who had many sheep. He took the pet sheep of a poor shepherd who had only one, killed it, and served it to a traveler for dinner.

David was angry with the rich man in the story. Completely absorbed and thoroughly disgusted, David pronounced to Nathan: "As surely as the LORD lives, the man who did this should die! He must pay for the lamb four times for doing such a thing. He had no mercy!" (verses 5–6 NCV).

At this moment Nathan, the courageous prophet, declared, "You are the man!.... You killed Uriah...and took his wife to become your wife" (verses 7, 9).

What daring accusations! What courage! But what would David's reaction be?

In the secrecy of his private world, David must have shuddered when Joab sent word that the murder of Uriah was accomplished. He must have confessed his sin a thousand times during the nine months of Bathsheba's pregnancy. As the baby grew in her womb, his conviction of sin must have grown, too. Referring to this period of time, which possibly lasted up to a year, David confessed:

"When I kept things to myself, I felt weak deep inside me. I moaned all day long. Day and night you punished me. My strength was gone as in the summer heat." (Psalm 32:3 4 NCV).

Now Nathan, a respected man of God, confronted and chastised him.. And David's reaction was "I have sinned against the LORD" (1 Samuel 12:13 NCV). Amazingly, along with the accusation came the positive word, "The LORD has taken away your sin" (verse 13). The confrontation resulted in acknowledgment of sin, brokenness, repentance, chastisement, and then restoration. Without a doubt, that was a wise and effective confrontation.

Do I really have to confront?

Very few people in this world enjoy confronting others about their sins, misunderstandings, or disagreements. (Those who really enjoy it should probably ask themselves why they do.) Most of us will go to any length necessary to avoid confrontation. Yet Scripture clearly says Christians should gently yet boldly confront other believers who sin against us or who are involved in wrongdoing. "If your brother sins, rebuke him, and if he repents, forgive him" (Luke 17:3).

Peter was confronted by both Jesus and Paul. Jesus had said to Peter, "Go away from me, Satan! You are not helping me! You don't care about the things of God, but only about the things people think are important" (Matthew 16:23 NCV). Later Paul said, "I spoke to Peter in front of them all. I said, 'Peter, you are a Jew, but you are not living like a Jew. You are living like those who are not Jewish. So why do you now try to force those who are not Jewish to live like Jews?'" (Galatians 2:14 NCV).

The confrontations had their desired effects. Peter became a great man of God and a encourager of the church.

Following Scripture

So often instead of talking to the offender, we talk to others behind his or her back. Besides involving others in troubles that are not theirs, we slander the reputation of our offenders. Then our anger grows, and we put ourselves into a position before others where we feel we can't back down. Or we use a wrong process to work out the problem.

A Brazilian Christian came into my office weeping. He said he had been mercilessly humiliated by a missionary in front of his colleagues.

My first reaction was like David's—empathy and anger. I had taken up other people's causes in the past and gotten in trouble for it. Foolishly, I was ready to do it again. But before I could do anything to compound the problem, I remembered Jesus' words.

....

If your fellow believer sins against you, go and tell him in private what he did wrong. If he listens to you, you have helped that person to be your brother or sister again. But if he refuses to listen, go to him again and take one or two other people with you. "Every case may be proved by two or three witnesses." If he refuses to listen to them, tell the church. If he refuses to listen to the church, then treat him like a person who does not believe in God or like a tax collector. (Matthew 18:15–20 NCV).

....

I read that passage to my friend and said, "I'm going to ask you to do the hardest thing you could possibly do. Go tell that man that he hurt you. Tell him how humiliated you felt. Then tell him that you are coming to forgive him; extend an invitation for him to acknowledge his sin and repent. If he doesn't respond as he should, you come back to me and we'll go together."

After he left my office, I prepared myself for the encounter that seemed inevitable. But when my friend returned a couple of hours later, he beamed and said, "I've won a brother."

A missionary once complained to me, "One of my board members is trying to walk off with the business. I've talked to him. Others have talked to him. It looks like I'll have to take him to court."

I did not want to see that happen. Scripture admonishes us not to take a brother to a civil court (1 Corinthians 6:1–11). So I said, "Why don't you take the matter to his church? Explain to the pastor that you have done everything you know to do and everything the Bible requires, but nothing has worked. Ask for his help."

Several weeks later, the missionary told me, "That was the best advice I ever received. The pastor got a group of leaders together and examined the situation, and the whole problem has been worked out."

When Paul exhorted the Galatian Christians to confront erring brothers, he gave them some guidelines:

··

If someone in your group does something wrong, you who are spiritual should go to that person and gently help him make him right again. But be careful, because you might be tempted to sin, too. By helping each other with your troubles, you truly obey the law of Christ.... Each person should judge his own actions (Galatians 6:1–2, 4 NCV).

··

"You who are spiritual…" Confrontation is clearly a job for those who are spiritually sensitive and whose lives are in order. Jesus said, "How can you say to your brother, 'Let me take the speck out of your eye,' when all the time there is a plank in your own eye?" (Matthew 7:4).

"Help make him right again." The objective is restoration, not just correction. If you don't have the right motive in mind, you are not ready to get involved.

"Gently…" So many situations are volatile. A harshly spoken or untrue word can cause an explosion that could put things out of place forever. "A gentle answer will calm a person's anger, but an unkind answer will cause more anger" (Proverbs 15:1 NCV).

"Helping each other." The Christian life wasn't designed to be lived alone. We need to be supportive, not judgmental, when our friends are struggling with sin in their lives.

"Each person should judge his own actions."
Beware of assuming a position of superiority.
Remember that no one is exempt from temptation. It
could be you next time.

I was part of a group of elders who brought together
two Christian brothers for reconciliation. One elder
clearly and compassionately stated the errors that one
of the men had committed and helped him to see
what he needed to do to correct his error.

In the course of the discussion, it became
apparent that I, as a leader, should have taken
action sooner, before the problem grew into a major
conflict.

The same elder then turned to me and said
lovingly, "George, you're my friend, and I love you.
But you let these situations go on too long. When
you see that a problem exists, you need to step in and
deal with it." My friend was right about my failure to
deal quickly with many issues, and he was right about
facing me with it. Christlike people lovingly confront
each other with the truth. It is a sign of maturity.

A case for confrontation

Richard Duncan, a former missionary in Brazil with
O.C. International and now a pastor in California, has
developed a series of studies concerning the ministry

of confrontation. He reminds us that confrontation is necessary when a person is headed for destruction. "Suppose I [God] say to the wicked: 'Wicked people, you will surely die,' but you don't speak to warn the wicked to stop doing evil. Then they will die because they were sinners but I will punish you for their deaths" (Ezekiel 33:8 NCV).

Then Duncan shares a series of tests, which I've adapted below, to decide whether the situation calls for confrontation.[1]

1. The test of love. Do I really care about this individual and want to help him? Do I love him enough to be patient, kind, and forgiving?

2. The test of truth. Do I know the truth about the situation? Is there specific Bible teaching about this issue?

3. The test of necessity. Is the situation serious enough to demand a confrontation? What will happen if the situation continues as it is?

4. The test of words. Have I thought this situation through so that I really know what I'm talking about? Does it call for some creativity like Nathan used?

5. The test of time. Is this the right time to deal with the situation? Is the person ready to face it? What kind of mood will I find the person in? How can I arrange the best possible circumstances that will contribute toward a successful encounter?

A wound that heals

The few people who love to confront often seem to enjoy a fight and take pleasure in showing their power. They can be cruel and sarcastic. "Why don't you grow up? Don't you get it? If you don't produce, you'll be fired. You're not irreplaceable, you know. Some people around here just don't carry their part of the load. Can't you do anything right? You're wrong; that's sin! How do you expect God to bless you when you act like that?"

Confronting in anger often does more harm than good. Still the errors that others commit in poor confrontations should not prevent us from doing what must be done. Confrontation can be done in a friendly way: "My brother, could I talk with you alone for a few minutes? I would like to share something I have noticed that you may not be aware of, and that could damage your relationship with the Lord and your ministry to others. Can we talk about it?"

David Augsburger points out that many see caring and confrontation as mutually exclusive. "There is a time for caring and a time for confrontation. To confront powerfully, lay care aside. To care genuinely, candor and confrontation must be forgotten for the moment at least."

Augsburger then suggests a third word: "Care-frontation unifies concern for relationship with concerns for goals, so one can have something to stand for (goals) as well as someone to stand with (relationships) without sacrificing one for the other or collapsing one with the other."[2]

Confrontation is not sign of animosity; it's a sign of true friendship, "It is better to correct someone openly than to have love and not show it. The slap of a friend can be trusted to help you, but the kisses of an enemy are nothing but lies" (Proverbs 27:5–6 NCV).

*A thief comes to steal and kill and destroy,
but I came to give life—life in all its fullness.*

JOHN 10:10 NCV

CHAPTER

14

It's Time to Live Abundantly

The abundant life that Jesus came to bring is to be lived *in the present tense*! It's not a life that "could have been" or "might someday be"; it's a life for here and now. It's not for an elite class of people; it's for you and me!

That said, abundant life doesn't come without a price. In the passage above, Jesus not only revealed what He came to provide *for* us; He also warned about what "the thief," Satan, comes to take *from* us. What a stark contrast we find between the two!

Satan	Jesus
Robs us.	Enriches us.
Cheats us.	Blesses us.
Brings us grief.	Brings us joy.
Deceives us.	Enlightens us.
Drives us.	Leads us.
Enslaves us.	Frees us.
Defeats us.	Empowers us.
Seeks to kill us.	Gives us life.

This promise of abundant life comes at the heart of a message in which Jesus calls himself the "Good Shepherd," who cares every day for his sheep: "He calls his own sheep by name and leads them out. When he brings all his sheep out, he goes ahead of them, and they follow him because they know his voice" (John 10:3–4 NCV).

The Good Shepherd knows us by name and loves us. He laid down his life for us. He calls us to abundant living. He promises to give us hope and a future and to satisfy our spiritual hunger.

What's the holdup?

So what keeps us from that life? Satan's opposition certainly does as do our lack of hearing, knowing, and following the voice of Jesus. Often, though, we fail to live the abundant life today because we are *reliving* negative experiences from yesterday and *dreading* or *avoiding* repetition of those experiences tomorrow.

Feelings of sorrow, guilt, shame, rejection, fear, anger, resentment, humiliation, and inadequacy chain us to the past and obstruct our future. Once memories fade or are repressed, we discover within ourselves negative responses and reactions that we still cannot explain to ourselves. Satan uses our past to effectively block the way to peace, freedom, victory, and the enjoyment of life here and now.

No going back!

If we could go back in time, we might attempt to avoid the errors we have committed and the painful things that have happened to us. But time tunnels work only in fiction. We may regret bad yesterdays and dream of better tomorrows, but our future is determined by what we do right now. Time alone doesn't heal. We need a powerful intervention in our lives that comes not from time but from eternity.

Here's the amazing news: The God who dwells in eternity allowed Himself to be compressed into time in the person of Jesus Christ, His Son, who experienced time as we do and offers us new life—abundant life!—always in the present tense.

If anyone is in Christ, he is a new creation; the old has gone, the new has come! (2 Corinthians 5:17).

Nothing is new without Jesus. With Him we have everything new—new standing, new birth, new life, new peace, new joy, new resilience, new security, new friendship—new life! In Him we are new creations. This new life begins with repentance. The word *repentance* is about change—changing our mind, behavior, allegiance, and direction. It's turning 180 degrees away from sin and turning to Jesus.

With that repentance comes forgiveness. The word *forgiveness* is about deciding that we are no longer going to maintain ill feelings, pay back, or even speak negatively about people who have hurt us. We accept forgiveness for ourselves and extend forgiveness to others.

When the Holy Spirit shows us our sin, we can confess and repent. When He reveals pain, we can forgive those who have caused it. When we bring closure to our past by confession and repentance or reconciliation, then we are ready to move on and receive God's promises. "The LORD says, 'Forget what happened before, and do not think about the past. Look at the new thing I am going to do.'" (Isaiah 43:18–19 NCV).

We can put our past behind us and live in the present enabled by God. We can and *will* see something new that will impact us positively and help us say *yes* to our future!

Today is the day!

Wouldn't it be wonderful to live without bitterness, anger, guilt, regrets, fear, addictions, and recurring bondages? Wouldn't we love to find healing for the complex, hurting people we have become?

God can change us now and continue that process. He can erase the marks our past has stamped upon us and break the chains that keep us repeating the "same old, same old" again and again. He can remake us into the victorious people He designed us to be. I love to think about this wonderful truth: God loves me just as I am, but He loves me too much to leave me as I am.

Let God reshape your life!

Jeremiah the prophet went to the potter's house to watch him work and said, "I saw him working at the wheel. But the pot he was shaping from the clay was marred in his hands; so the potter formed it into another pot, shaping it as seemed best to him" (Jeremiah 18:3–4).

Even though the vessel broke, it never left the potter's hand. He remade it into something beautiful— just as God wants to do with you and me. Even when we feel that our lives have fallen apart, God has a plan for us. He never gives up. The God who began a good work in you "will continue it until it is finished" (Philippians 1:6 NCV).

Grace to get on with life

Today can be the deciding day. You can resign yourself to defeat and unhappiness, or you can choose the abundant life. I offer you six truths to help you start living the abundant life that God intends for you here and now.

1. Know that Jesus wants to forgive and heal and restore you! No matter what you have done, He can forgive you! No matter what you have suffered, He can heal you! "God began doing a good work in you, and I am sure he will continue it until it is finished" (Philippians 1:6 NCV).

2. Choose recovery. Sure, there are people you could blame, but what good does it do? People may attack you, but they cannot destroy you. "If God is for us, no one can defeat us" (Romans 8:31 NCV). God will put your life back together if you do your part.

3. Commit your whole life to Christ. If you have never received Jesus as your Lord and Savior, do it now. Entrust your life to His care and service. "Yet to all who received him, to those who believed in his name, he gave the right to become children of God" (John 1:12).

4. Ask for and extend forgiveness. Admit your wrongdoing and ask forgiveness. As you recall your pain, forgive those who caused it. "Confess your sins to each other and pray for each other so that you may be healed" (James 5:16 NLT).

5. Follow through. Even after facing your issues, you may be tempted to relive the hurts or blame individuals. Replace those thoughts with these: *I have forgiven this person. I no longer blame him or her for my situation. I have been forgiven, too, so I no longer blame myself. I will trust God and move on.* By forgiving, you replace hostility with love and anxiety with faith, and you are freed from your past. "God's peace...will keep your hearts and minds in Christ Jesus" (Philippians 4:7 NCV).

6. Reclaim ground from Satan. Scripture warns of the harmful effects of sustained anger: "When you are angry, do not sin, and be sure to stop being angry before the end of the day. Do not give the devil a way to defeat you" (Ephesians 4:26–27 NCV).

This time-tested and proven process demands faith and courage, but Jesus will help you stand on the forgiveness and acceptance you have in Him. And He will help you grant the same forgiveness to others. Leave your hurts in the past and make abundant living a present reality. God bless you!

NOTES

Chapter 2
1. David Seamands, "The Hidden Tormentors" (sermon, Wilmore United Methodist Church, Wilmore, KY, date unknown).

Chapter 4
1. LeRoy Dugan, "Message of the Cross" (Minneapolis: Bethany International, Oct Dec 1994), 14.

Chapter 5
1. Bruce Wilkinson, *Secrets of the Vine*, (Sisters, OR: Multnomah Press), 71.

Chapter 6
1. R. T. Kendall, *Total Forgiveness* (Lake Mary, FL: Charisma House, 2002), 20.
2. Ibid., 183–184.

Chapter 8
1. Corrie ten Boom with Jamie Buckingham, *Tramp for the Lord, Special Crusade Edition* (Fort Washington, PA: Christian Literature Crusade, and Old Tappan, NJ: Fleming H. Revell, 1974), 56.
2. Ibid., 179–180.

Chapter 9
1. Corrie ten Boom with Jamie Buckingham, *Tramp for the Lord,* Special Crusade Edition (Fort Washington,

PA: Christian Literature Crusade, and Old Tappan, NJ: Fleming H. Revell, 1974), 181–182.

Chapter 10

1. Robert Lowry, "Nothing but the Blood" (1875).
2. R. T. Kendall, *How to Forgive Ourselves—Totally*, (Lake Mary, FL: Charisma House, 2007), 17–30.
3. David Seamands, "The Hidden Tormentors" (sermon, Wilmore United Methodist Church, Wilmore, KY, date unknown.

Chapter 11

1. Caio Fábio d'Araújo Filho, *Perdão, Encarnação da Graça* [Forgiveness, Incarnation of Grace], (Niteroi, RJ, Brazil: Editora Vinde, 1990).

Chapter 13

1. Richard Duncan, *Passo a Passo* [Step byStep] (São Paulo: Sepal, 1990), 89–90.
2. David Augsburger, *The Love Fight* (Scottsdale, PA: Herald Press, 1983), 9.